Eyewitness
SEASHORE

Sugar kelp

Bladder wrack

Dog whelk

Dogfish eggcases
containing embryos

Hebrew cone shells

Carragheen

Dulse

Common cormorant

Rock oyster

Eyewitness
SEASHORE

In association with
THE NATURAL HISTORY MUSEUM

Written by
STEVE PARKER

Cushion stars

Common prawn

Spiny starfish

Brittlestar

Rock sea lavender

A Dorling Kindersley Book

Guillemot eggs

Pine cone

Dried seaweed

DK

LONDON, NEW YORK, MUNICH,
MELBOURNE, and DELHI

Project editor Elizabeth Eyres
Art editor Miranda Kennedy
Senior editor Sophie Mitchell
Managing editor Sue Unstead
Managing art editor Roger Priddy
Special photography Dave King
Editorial consultants
The staff of the
Natural History Museum, London

PAPERBACK EDITION
Managing editor Andrew Macintyre
Managing art editor Jane Thomas
Senior editor Kitty Blount
Senior art editor Martin Wilson
Editor Karen O'Brien
Art Editor Ann Cannings
Production Jenny Jacoby
Picture research Lorna Ainger
DTP designer Siu Yin Ho

Snakelocks anemone

This Eyewitness ® Guide has been conceived by
Dorling Kindersley Limited and Editions Gallimard

Hardback edition first published in Great Britain in 1989.
This edition pubished in Great Britain in 2003
by Dorling Kindersley Limited,
80 Strand, London WC2R 0RL

A CIP catalogue record for this book is
available from the British Library.

ISBN 978-0-7513-6479-8

Color reproduction by Colourscan, Singapore
Printed in China by Toppan Printing Co. (Shenzhen) Ltd.

Gull feathers

Limpet

Pipefish

See our complete
catalogue at

www.dk.com

Contents

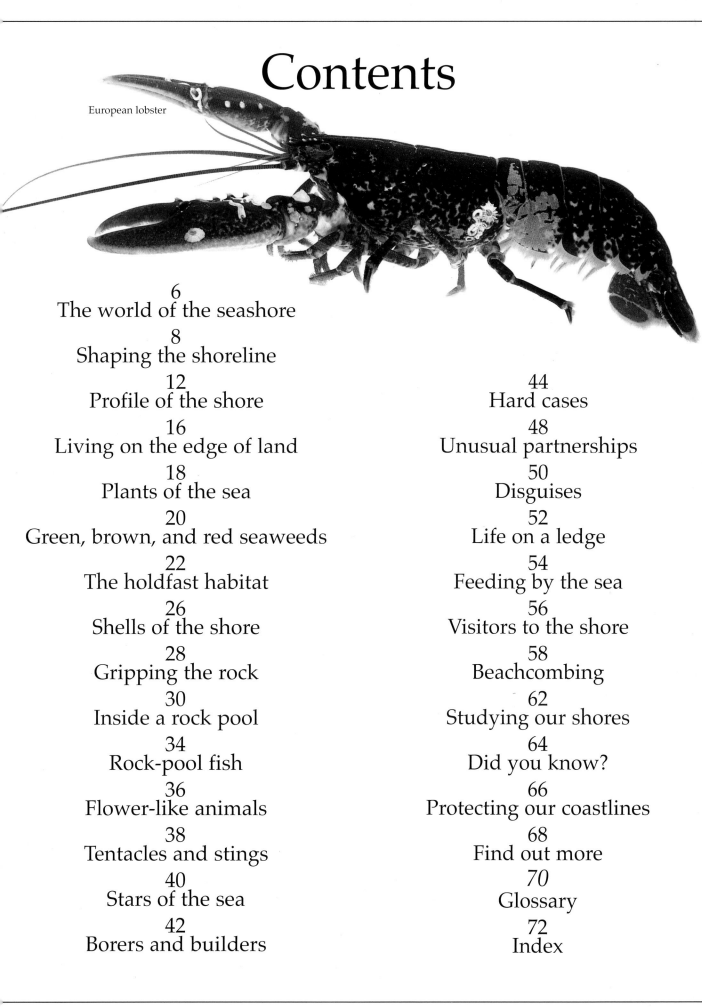

European lobster

The world of the seashore

TWO-THIRDS OF OUR PLANET is covered with water. Every fragment of land, from the great continent of Eurasia to the tiniest Pacific island, has a shore. The total length of shorelines is huge. Yet the width is hardly measurable in comparison - it is often just a few metres. Shores are peculiar places, being the edge of the land as well as the edge of the sea. The sea level rises and falls with the tides, making the shore sometimes wet and sometimes dry. Winds drive unfettered across the open ocean and hit the coast with great force. As they blow, they whip up waves that endlessly crash into the land. No two stretches of shore are the same. Each is shaped by many variable factors - the tides, winds, waves, water currents, temperature, and climate, and the types of rock from which the land is made. Along each shore a group of highly adapted plants and animals - many of them strange to our land-orientated eyes - make their homes. This book explores the world of the seashore and describes how its inhabitants adapt to their constantly changing surroundings.

Shaping the shoreline

F OR MILLIONS OF YEARS, every few seconds of each day, waves have hit the seashore. Generated and driven by wind, in calm weather they may be slight ripples, but in a fresh breeze they tumble in foaming heaps on to rocks or sandy beach. In a storm, great breakers pound the substance of the shore like massive hammer-blows. Waves erode the shore in three different ways. One is by the hydraulic pressure they exert as they move up the shore and then crash down upon it as they break. A second is by the pneumatic pressure created as water is hurled against rock. It traps pockets of air that are forced into every tiny crack and fissure, rather like a compressed-air gun. In this way small crevices are widened, and tunnels may be forced along joints in the rock of a low cliff and out at the top, forming blow-holes through which each wave shoots spray-laden air. The third way in which waves wear away the land is by corrasion. This is the grinding action of the rocks of all sizes - from giant boulders to tiny sand grains - that are picked up by the waves and flung against the shore. Under this constant barrage, no coastline can remain untouched.

WHO'S WINNING?
The sea is gradually wearing away the land on some stretches of coast. But the land may be slowly rising, too - making the struggle more even. Plants such as marram grass help to reduce erosion on sand dunes by binding the grains with their roots and creating sheltered pockets where other plants can grow.

ON THE WAY TO SAND
The sea gradually wears down large blocks of stone into boulders, then into pebbles, like these, then into sand grains, and finally to tiny particles of silt.

POUNDING SURF
Waves exert tremendous force as they crash on to the coast. The weight of sea slapping the shore every few seconds can create pressures of more than 25 tonnes (tons) per square metre (yard) - 30 times the pressure under your foot as you stand.

RISING TIDE
Time and tide wait for no one, especially picnickers at the seaside who have failed to keep an eye on the water level.

| Sun | Moon | Bulge of water | Earth |

FORCES FROM SPACE
Twice each day the sea rises up the shore and then recedes. These movements of water are called tides and are caused by the Moon and, to a lesser extent, the Sun pulling the Earth's water towards them, creating a bulge. When the Sun and Moon are in line, as shown above, the bulge is most pronounced and the tides are at their highest and lowest (p. 12).

As hard as rock?

The type of rock of which the shore is made is one of the chief factors governing the nature of a coastline. Hard rocks such as granites, basalts, and some sandstones are resistant to erosion, and often form high headlands and tall, stable cliffs on which plants can gain a footing (p. 16).

Granite coloured pink by the mineral orthoclase

COARSE OF GRAIN
Granite is entirely an igneous rock, that is, it is formed as molten rock cools and the different minerals in it crystallize. Its crystals are relatively large; granite is said to be coarse-grained.

Granite tinted white by the mineral plagioclase

VARIABLE IN COLOUR
As granite is worn by the sea and the weather, its less-resistant mineral parts, such as feldspar, change to softer clay-like substances. The quartz and mica mineral particles are much harder: they become separated from the soft clay and may eventually become sand on a beach.

VOLCANIC ISLANDS
This lava, from the island of Madeira off northwest Africa, is full of holes created by bubbles of gas trapped as the rock solidified.

LAVA COAST
Some parts of the coast are formed of dark lava flows such as these on the island of Hawaii.

Hexagonal columns created by cooling pattern in basalt

Mainland sandstone cliff

NATURAL COLUMNS
Basalt is another hard igneous rock. It is sometimes worn into startling geometric columns, such as this 70-m (230-ft) deep cave on the west coast of Scotland, which is known as Fingal's Cave, and the huge "stepping stones" of the Giant's Causeway in Ireland.

Isolated stack of sandstone formed by the collapse of bridge joining it to mainland (p. 10)

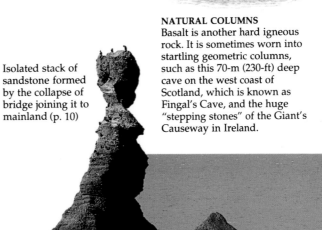

ONCE A BEACH
The grains show clearly in this sample of sandstone. Perhaps on an ancient beach they settled, were cemented together, and then were lifted by huge movements of the Earth's crust, and now lie exposed again on a coastal cliff.

Rocks from ancient seas

Many softer rocks, such as chalk and limestone, are sedimentary in origin. They were formed when small particles of calcite, which were largely the remains of plants and animals, settled out as sediment on the bottom of an ancient sea. More particles settled on top, and those underneath were gradually squeezed and cemented by chemicals into solid rock. Sometimes whole plants and animals were trapped in the sediments and these were gradually turned into rock to become fossils.

DISAPPEARING CLIFF
Shores made of soft material such as sand, clay, and other loose particles may be quickly worn down by waves, and material carried away by currents. On some stretches of shore, wooden barriers called groynes are built to reduce the amount of sediment removed by currents.

WORK OF THE WAVES
As waves approach a headland, they are bent so that they crash into its sides. Headlands made of well-jointed rocks such as sandstones and limestones may have their lower sides eroded completely causing an arch to form. In time this becomes a "tower" of rock called a stack.

THE END OF THE ROAD
Where the coastal rock is soft and crumbly, whole seaside communities have been swallowed by the sea. This road led originally to some houses, whose ruins are now under the waves.

SLOW TO CHANGE
This fossilized brittlestar (p. 40) was found at the foot of a cliff. It lived some 200 million years ago, but is very similar to those living today.

GROOVED "PEBBLES"
Hard shells make good fossils. These "pebbles" are brachiopods, or lampshells, which are similar to shellfish like cockles (p. 26). They are common in many sedimentary rocks and help to date the rocks.

STONE BULLETS
These are the fossilized internal shells of belemnites, prehistoric squid-like molluscs.

Stalks of sea-lilies

TENTACLE TRACERY
This tracery is a bed of fossilized crinoids or sea-lilies, which lived 200 million years ago. Crinoids are animals related to starfish (p. 40).

WHITE CLIFFS

Chalk is a type of limestone, often dazzling white in colour, which may form tall cliffs. Here the various strata (layers) laid down at different times can be seen. At the foot of the cliff, lumps eroded from above are found with pebbles brought by currents from other parts of the coast.

Strata (layers) of chalk laid down at the bottom of an ancient sea

ANCIENT SEA LIFE

Chalk is made of fragments of fossilized microscopic sea plants and animals. Large fossils such as mollusc shells are sometimes embedded in it.

SOLID MUD

Shale is a soft rock which splits easily along the layers in which it was laid down and is quickly eroded where it is exposed at the coast. Types that contain the decomposed remains of sea plants and animals are known as oil shale. When heated, oil shale releases a type of crude oil. It may become an important natural resource in the future.

Fossilized shells in limestone

ONCE A SEA-BED

Limestone sometimes forms breathtaking cliffs, arches, and stacks. This is the 200-m (650-ft) high plateau of the Nullarbor Plain, in southern Australia, which itself was once a sea-bed. Limestone is a sedimentary rock, often rich in fossils. Lumps may fall from the cliff and split open to reveal remains of prehistoric animals and plants.

Limestone pebbles worn smooth by rubbing against other pebbles on the shore

Profile of the shore

No TWO COASTS are quite the same. But a naturalist can look at an unfamiliar shore (especially a rocky one) and tell at a glance how high the tide rises, how low it falls, whether the area is exposed to wind and waves, or whether it is sheltered. The journey from the edge of the land to the beginning of the sea passes through a series of bands or zones, each with characteristic animals and plants that need to be covered by the sea for different lengths of time. The highest band is the splash or spray zone, which is above the high-water level of the highest tides and is occasionally drenched by spray. Land plants and animals that are adapted to salty conditions live here. Lichens, which are fungi and algae growing in partnership, are found here as well as a few straying sea-snails (p. 26). The lower limit of the splash zone is generally marked by barnacles (p. 44), the first truly marine creatures. The next band is the intertidal ("between the tides") zone, which is regularly covered and uncovered by water. It extends from the barnacles down through the wrack seaweeds (pp. 20-21) to the low-tide area, where larger kelp seaweeds (pp. 22-25) begin to take over. The third broad band is the subtidal ("below the tides") zone, stretching from the kelp fringe into the permanent shallows.

SAND BINDER
Sea sandwort's creeping stems and tough roots help it to stabilize loose soil on sand and shingle.

SALT'S INCREASING INFLUENCE
The influence of salt water increases from the cliff top, occasionally splashed by storm spray, down through layers that are regularly splashed or sometimes immersed, to the permanently submerged subtidal zone. Different plants and animals are found in each zone.

High-water mark
of spring tides

THE HIGHEST HIGH TIDE
Every two weeks, the Moon and Sun are in line with the Earth. At this time they exert their maximum gravitational pulls on the sea, and so cause the greatest "bulge" of water (p. 8). This produces the highest high tides and the lowest low tides. They are called spring tides.

High-water mark
of average tides

AVERAGE HIGH TIDE
The upper shore lies around and just below the average high-tide mark, at the upper fringe of the intertidal zone. The high-tide mark itself progresses up the beach during the course of a week, finally reaching the spring-tide level. Then it moves gradually back down over the next week. On the upper shore, animals and plants are usually covered by water for one to two hours in each tidal cycle, although on a spring high tide they may be immersed for longer.

BARNACLED BOTTOMS
Feathery-limbed barnacles (right) will settle on any stable surface, including the hulls of ships. Their crusty fouling growths are a problem, as they slow a ship's speed. Anti-fouling paints have been developed for hulls, containing chemicals that stop young barnacles settling.

A barnacle extends its feathery limbs to grasp and draw food into its mouth, inside the shell plates

FIGHTING IN SLOW MOTION
Limpets are found throughout the intertidal zone. Some species guard territories to protect their food - a green "garden" of algae (p. 18). Here a light-coloured limpet strays on to a neighbour's territory; the occupant crawls over and wedges its shell under the intruder, who then slides away defeated.

Barnacles

The middle and lower shore is on pages 14-15

SPRINGY TURF
Well above the high-tide mark, the matted roots of grasses hold the soil and help to prevent erosion.

Pockets of soil build up in cracks and hollows at the back of the shore

SHINY JUICY DROPLETS
Common and adaptable, thorny bramble stems trail along the back of the shore and bear late-summer blackberry fruits.

YELLOW FLOWERS
The horned poppy adorns shingle, sandy flats, and cliffs with its bright-yellow summer flowers.

Grey mosaic of Lecanora

Greyish-green tufts of Ramalina

PAINTED ROCKS
Rocks around and above high-tide mark often bear fine growths of coloured lichens. Each likes different amounts of light, spray, and exposure in that area.

Yellow branches of Xanthoria

Rough periwinkle

Channelled wrack is one of the highest-growing seaweeds, at home on the upper shore and even above high-tide level, if regularly covered in spray

Common limpet

Blackish stain of Verrucaria

THE LOWEST HIGH TIDE
Alternating with the fortnightly spring tides are the neap tides. When the Moon and Sun are at right angles, their gravitational pulls cancel each other out, so there is no very high or very low tide. Any stationary form of life that requires at least a few minutes' immersion on each tide cannot live above the neap high-tide level.

High-water
mark of neap tides

The limpet Patella aspera *is found on the middle and lower shore*

HARSH LICKERS
Purple topshells crawl among the wrack sea-weeds on the middle shore, scraping off tiny algal growths with their file-like tongues.

ROVER ON THE SHORE
The predatory dog whelk roves over most of the shore, feeding on mussels and barnacles.

KELP FANCIERS
These painted topshells graze on the kelp seaweeds of the lower shore.

NO WET FEET
Mussels live in estuaries and on more exposed rocky shores, generally on the lower shore below the barnacle belt. Collecting them during spring low tides avoids getting the feet wet.

OYSTER BORE
The sting winkle feeds by boring through oyster, mussel, and barnacle shells to reach the flesh.

FIXED ATTACHMENT
The saddle oyster attaches itself to lower-shore and offshore rocks.

THE HIGHEST LOW TIDE
Just as neap high tides do not reach very far up the shore, so neap low tides do not run very far down. The tidal range at neaps may be less than half of the range at springs.

Low-water
mark of neap tides

AVERAGE LOW TIDE
The lower shore lies around and just above the average low-tide mark, at the lower fringe of the intertidal zone. Here, life can be sure of always being covered during the neap-tide period.

Low-water
mark of average tides

Large brown kelps are only uncovered at the low water of spring tides

THE BARNACLE BELT
As exposure to wind and waves increases away from shelter, so the wrack seaweeds have trouble surviving. Their place on the upper and middle rocky shore is taken by the barnacles, which form a distinct belt along many coasts. On some Australian shores, there are more than 120,000 barnacles to the square metre (yard).

Barnacles

SEABORNE FOOD
Many fixed creatures, such as these horse mussels, rely on the sea to bring them food in the form of tiny floating particles.

Mussels encrusted with barnacles and sea-mats

TIDE RIGHT OUT
The best time to study the rocky shore is at low spring tide (p. 63).

Living on the edge of land

THE EDGE OF LAND
Many of the world's people live on or near coasts. The higher and rockier a shoreline, the fewer people visit it and as a result a greater variety of wildlife is found there.

APPROACHING THE COAST from inland, we notice how conditions change. There is usually more wind - the sea breeze blows unrestricted across the open ocean. There is also a salty tang to the air, as tiny droplets of seawater are blown off the waves by the wind. Plants growing near the shore must be able to cope with strong winds and, if they are in the splash zone, salt spray. They tend to be low-growing to avoid the full force of the wind. Another problem for plants, especially on shingle and on stony cliff tops, is shortage of water. Rain soon dries in the breeze or trickles away between the rocks. Some species, such as rock samphire, have thick, fleshy, tough-skinned leaves that store plenty of reserve water. A number of plants that are found on the coast are well adapted to dry habitats and may also grow under similar conditions inland.

ROCK-DWELLING LAVENDER
Rock sea lavender is a close relative of the sea lavender of saltmarshes, but it is quite unrelated to lavender itself.

EVERLASTING THRIFT
Sea pink is another name for thrift, which grows in a cushion as protection against the wind. It retains its colour when dried and is a favourite with flower-arrangers.

Fleshy leaves

Fruit

AT HOME ON STONE
Stonecrops really do grow in dense mats (crops) among stones. After they have flowered, reddish-brown fruits are left on the flowering stems.

SEASIDE MAYWEED
The sea mayweed has daisy-like flowers and fleshy leaves. It flowers in late summer (not May), and is characteristic of stony ground such as wastelands, shingle, and undercliffs.

FROM FLOWER TO FRUIT

The tiny, fluffy-looking, yellow-green midsummer flowers of rock samphire have faded and are now developing into brown, "corky" fruits. The juicy leaves of this coastal plant were eaten in the past, either pickled or lightly cooked and served with butter.

Fruit

Each flower has five tiny petals

Fleshy leaves covered by tough skin

Tiny oil glands on undersurfaces of leaves

RED OR WHITE

Red valerian sometimes has white or pink flowers. It is found in rocky places: by the coast on cliffs and shingle and inland on stone walls.

CUSHION OF THYME

Wild thyme is not confined to the coast - it also grows in other dry habitats, such as sand dunes, heaths, and cliff tops. It has low, creeping stems and it flowers throughout the summer. Like its cultivated relative, wild thyme has a distinctive sweet and pungent scent which comes from its natural aromatic oil, thymol.

A collection of scurvy grasses

ANTLER LEAVES

Plantains are mostly tough, stringy, low-growing plants, as gardeners well know. The buck's horn plantain is named after its branched antler-like leaves and is common in many coastal areas.

FULL OF VITAMINS

Scurvy grass leaves are rich in vitamin C and were eaten by sailors to ward off the disease scurvy. It is not a grass but a member of the cabbage family.

WITHERED BY WIND

Most trees struggle to grow in the windy, salt-laden conditions on cliff tops. This oak has been bent and withered by the wind.

Plants of the sea

ALONG THE SHORE - and in the sea itself - are plants quite unlike the familiar trees and flowers of the land. Seaweeds is the common term, and indeed these plants grow like weeds along many coasts. They are also known as algae. Unlike garden weeds the algae do not develop flowers and then set seed. They reproduce in a variety of ways, some by means of swollen tips which release male and female cells into the water. The algae have no roots, stems, or leaves like land plants; instead the larger types have stipes (stems) and fronds (leaves), and sometimes root-like anchoring holdfasts (pp. 22-23). Most algae also lack a network of tube-like "plumbing" to transport water and dissolved nutrients throughout the plant. Instead they absorb nutrients through their surface directly from seawater. The three groups found on rocky shores are green, brown, and red seaweeds.

FEATHERY FRONDS
The delicate structure of many red seaweeds, such as this common *Plocamium*, is best seen when submerged. Red seaweeds add splashes of colour to the lower shore and shallows.

SEAWEEDS AT HOME
Seaweeds are difficult to keep in aquariums. Marine salts can help to make "imitation" seawater but most seaweeds also need constant water movement bringing fresh nutrients and oxygen, and regular tidal cycles that submerge and expose them.

GREEN RIBBONS
Several similar species of *Enteromorpha* thrive on rocky shores. They also grow in estuaries or where a freshwater stream runs over the rocks making the water less salty.

Enteromorpha

INVADER ON THE SHORE
Japanese sargassum has found its way to the British south coast, the USA, and elsewhere. It was probably introduced with oyster spat (spawn) imported from Japan. In some areas this brown seaweed is altering the shore's ecology. Closely related to this plant are the dense masses of floating weed that form in the Sargasso Sea and are occasionally washed on to our shores.

Japanese sargassum

RICH PICKINGS
Shore birds will eat seaweeds, such as *Enteromorpha* and *Ulva*, and will also snap up the small animals sheltering under them. Several species of birds make a living by searching through seaweed beds during low tide.

RED-FEATHERED ROCK DWELLER
Featherweed is a rich crimson-red seaweed found anchored to rocks in shaded places on the middle and lower shore. Its body branches successively into feathery tufts.

SIGN OF SUMMER
In spring and summer this branching brown seaweed, *Bifurcaria*, bears spotty, swollen tips, which contain its reproductive structures. The species is found in pools on the middle and lower shore, where it is always covered by water.

Bifurcaria

BREADCRUMB SPONGE
Attached to the rock near the hair-like *Spongomorpha* weed is a deep-green sponge. This is the common breadcrumb sponge, found in shady gulleys and under boulders on the lower shore. Sponges are primitive animals that draw in water from which they extract oxygen and floating particles of food.

Water passes into the sponge through tiny holes and passes out through the larger, visible holes

Red seaweed growing on Bifurcaria

Spongomorpha (left)

Developing swollen tips contain reproductive structures

Channelled wrack

MARKING HIGH WATER
Dry-looking bunches of channelled wrack hang from rocks along the upper shore, often marking the high-water line. This plant gets its name from the channels or grooves along its fronds.

COLOURFUL CORALWEED
There are many types of coralline weed or coralweed along the shore. These red seaweeds lay down a chalky deposit. They grow in rock pools and shady places from the middle shore downwards.

Coralweed

HAIR WEED
This is one type of *Cladophora*, a common hair-like green seaweed with a branching structure found up and down the shore.

Featherweed

Cladophora

19

Green, brown, and red seaweeds

THE MOST OBVIOUS seaweeds on the shore are usually the large brown seaweeds known as wracks and kelps. Wracks are leathery strap-like seaweeds that grow in bands between the high- and low-tide marks. Some species have air bladders that keep the main body (the thallus) of the weed afloat as the waves come and go. The kelps have much broader blade-like fronds and tend to live around the low-water mark and below. Red seaweeds are generally smaller and prefer shady rock pools and deeper water beyond the kelp zone. They contain a red pigment, phycoerythrin, that masks out the green pigment chlorophyll, which is present in all plants. This is more efficient at using the dim light filtering through seawater than the fucoxanthin pigment of the brown seaweeds. This means that the reds are able to grow at greater depths than other seaweeds.

FROM HIGH TO LOW
On rocky shores seaweeds are found in horizontal bands or zones. These bands of bright-green seaweeds, greenish-brown wracks, red seaweeds, and brown kelps at the low-tide mark form a basic pattern which is repeated, with variations in the species, all over the world.

Air pocket

SWOLLEN TIPS
A mature bladder wrack has swollen tips containing reproductive organs.

POCKETS OF AIR
Some specimens of bladder wrack develop large air pockets in pairs along the central midrib of the frond as here. Yet other specimens, especially from exposed coasts, have few or even no bladders. No one knows why this is so.

Serrated wrack

Sea lettuce

SEAWEED SALAD
left and above
Sea lettuce, which looks a lot like the plant we eat in salads, can grow in many different habitats - in the slightly salty water of estuaries, in seawater, and even in mildly polluted waters. This green seaweed is very common. It can be found attached to rocks, floating freely, or washed up on shore.

WEED WITH TEETH
Toothed or serrated wrack is named after the saw-like teeth along the edges of its fronds. It is a member of the Fucus group, but unlike its close relatives it has no air bladders.

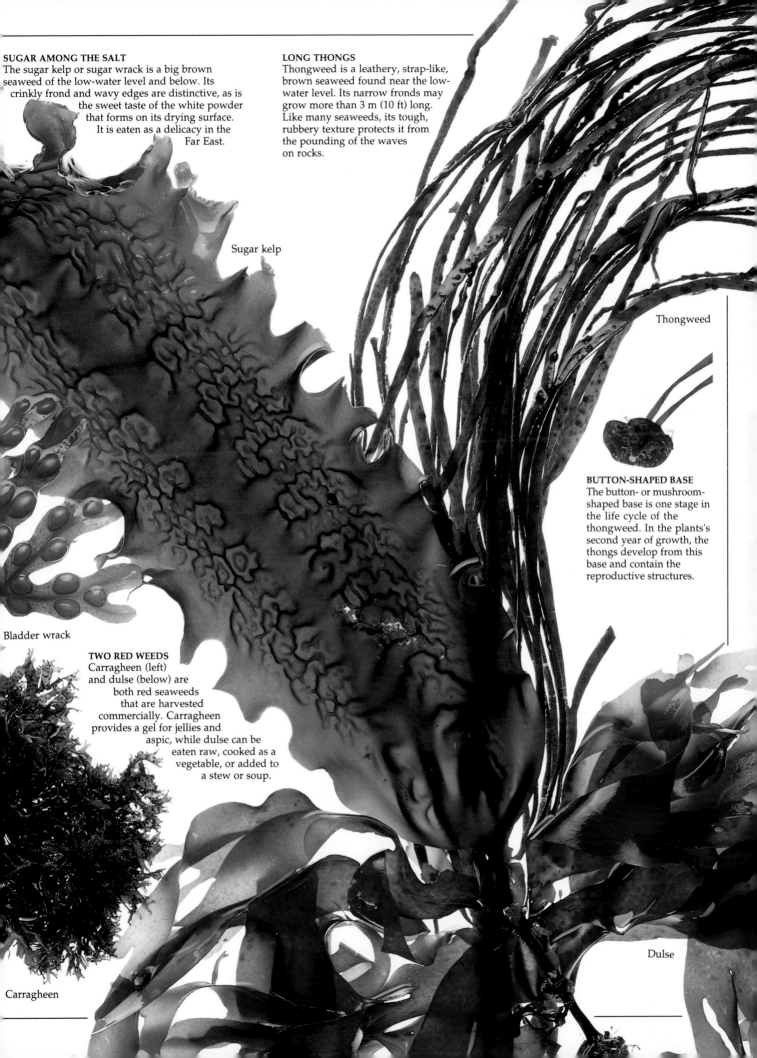

SUGAR AMONG THE SALT
The sugar kelp or sugar wrack is a big brown seaweed of the low-water level and below. Its crinkly frond and wavy edges are distinctive, as is the sweet taste of the white powder that forms on its drying surface. It is eaten as a delicacy in the Far East.

Sugar kelp

LONG THONGS
Thongweed is a leathery, strap-like, brown seaweed found near the low-water level. Its narrow fronds may grow more than 3 m (10 ft) long. Like many seaweeds, its tough, rubbery texture protects it from the pounding of the waves on rocks.

Thongweed

BUTTON-SHAPED BASE
The button- or mushroom-shaped base is one stage in the life cycle of the thongweed. In the plants's second year of growth, the thongs develop from this base and contain the reproductive structures.

Bladder wrack

TWO RED WEEDS
Carragheen (left) and dulse (below) are both red seaweeds that are harvested commercially. Carragheen provides a gel for jellies and aspic, while dulse can be eaten raw, cooked as a vegetable, or added to a stew or soup.

Carragheen

Dulse

The holdfast habitat

SEAWEEDS do not have true roots. The gnarled, root-like structures of large brown seaweeds are called, appropriately, holdfasts. They hold tight to the rock and provide anchorage, like a tree's roots in the soil. Unlike true roots, the rootlets of a holdfast do not take up water or nutrients; instead these are absorbed through the whole surface of the seaweed. However, holdfasts do provide shelter on the shore. Just as trees protect a woodland's interior from wind, driving rain, and hot sun, so the leathery fronds and tough holdfasts of the low-shore kelp forests keep off the sun and lessen the force of waves and winds. Many smaller plants and numerous shore animals, such as crabs, fish, prawns, and molluscs, take advantage of the calmer conditions within the forests of brown seaweeds. During storms, weaker seaweeds are torn from the rocks. In the storm's aftermath, huge mounds of kelp are found on the shore, often with their inhabitants still clinging to the fronds. The Californian sea-otter (p.56) is a well-known inhabitant of the kelp beds of the Pacific coast. When it rests on the surface, it secures itself by wrapping kelp fronds around its body.

Mussels indicate that the seaweed is at least several years old

HOLDING FAST
Oarweeds, sometimes called cuvie or forest kelp, grip firmly to the rock with the finger-like rootlets of their holdfasts. Other brown seaweeds, as well as red and green species, have colonized this small piece of slate. Their bases have grown into every crack and cranny in the rock.

Young oarweeds

FLATTENED KELP DWELLER
The porcelain crab is a filter-feeder and more closely related to hermit crabs (pp. 48-49) and lobsters than true crabs. Its walking legs have sharp spines that allow it to grip apparently smooth rock or slippery holdfasts with ease, sliding its flat body under boulders or into hollows among the holdfast rootlets.

Porcelain crab

CUTAWAY HIDEAWAY
A section cut through the side of a holdfast (right) shows its tough and stringy structure. It also reveals a tiny "cave" where the porcelain crab (above) shelters.

FRILLS AND FURBELOWS
One of the most distinctive brown seaweeds is furbelows. Its stipe has elaborately waved edges and divides into long fan-like fronds that may grow to 2 m (6 ft) or more.

DRYING THE SHORE'S HARVEST
Seaweeds are nutritious plants, being especially rich in some vitamins and minerals such as iodine. In many regions they are eaten regularly as a vegetable-like dish or chopped and grated as garnish. In Japan kelp and laver (a red seaweed) are cultivated and sold as kombu and nori respectively.

Hollow underside

Furbelows

Rootlets of holdfast

PLANT OR PLASTIC?
Like other large kelps, furbelows grows at the low-tide level and below. Its bloated holdfast, covered in wart-like growths resembling bubble-filled plastic packaging, grows in one year, for this plant is an annual.

TUG'O'WAR WITH THE WAVES
Similar species of coastal kelps are found around the world. This holdfast anchors a *Macrocystis* (a type of giant kelp) from New Zealand. The entire plant is tens of metres long. Waves and water currents pull on the enormous fronds with great force, so the holdfast must be equal to the challenge. More than 600 species of seaweeds have been recorded in New Zealand waters.

☞

The rest of the kelp is shown on the next page

A SHARP TONGUE
Blue-rayed limpets are common grazers on kelps, rasping away at the seaweed itself and any encrusting plants and animals. Sometimes this mollusc erodes a "home base" (p. 29) in the holdfast.

Red seaweeds growing on kelp

Porcelain crab in hollow of holdfast

CLEANING THE KELP
The common sea-urchin is one of
many shore creatures that graze
the rocks and weeds. Using its
powerful jaws (p. 28), the urchin
scrapes the rocks and kelp stipes
clean, consuming small algal
growths and tiny settled animals.
Occasionally plagues of urchins
occur and strip away all new
growth from the rocks, leaving
them bare and lifeless.

*Blade base splits
into fronds*

Stipe of kelp

GIANT WEEDS
A *Macrocystis* or
giant kelp from
California that is the home
of the sea-otter (p. 56). Some
types of giant kelp may grow 1 m
(3 ft) in a day under good conditions, and
reach lengths of 100 m (over 300 ft).

Ends of fronds are decaying

Scar tissue formed over wounds caused by feeding animals

Coastal rowers may get their oars entangled in the oarweed forests

LACY MATS
The delicate lacy patterns seen on some kelps are sea-mats. Each growth consists of many tiny creatures, similar to sea-anemones, in miniature limy boxes.

Dogfish lay their eggs among seaweed (p. 61)

Shells of the shore

SHE SELLS SEA SHELLS
The beauty and hardness of sea shells has made them favourites for jewellery, and for fancy goods such as the decorative shell boxes sold by the little girl in the picture. In some coastal areas, certain shells were used as currency, such as the "money cowries" of tropical islands.

ON THE SEASHORE many of the animals that live inside shells are molluscs. They are commonly known as shellfish. Molluscs are an enormous and varied animal group, with over 120,000 species worldwide. The typical mollusc has a soft body, a muscular foot on which it moves, and a hard shell made of calcium carbonate and other minerals extracted from seawater; but there are many variations. On the shore, the group includes gastropods (snail-like molluscs) such as limpets, abalones, topshells, nerites, winkles, conches, whelks, cowries, and cone shells.

Most of the edible molluscs are bivalves, which have two parts, or valves, to the shell. These include cockles, mussels, scallops, clams, oysters, razorshells, and shipworms. Tusk shells, chitons, sea-slugs, squid, and octopuses also belong to the mollusc group.

Eight jointed shell plates

TEETH OF IRON
Chitons, or coat-of-mail shells (p. 28) are common molluscs on many rocky shores, but are difficult to spot as they blend in with the rocks. This species is a mid-shore seaweed-grazer from the Indian Ocean. Its tiny teeth are capped with a hard, iron-containing substance that prevents them from becoming worn.

STRIPES AND SPOTS
Topshells, with their striped and spotted cone-shaped shells, are bright and familiar inhabitants of rock pools (pp. 30-33). This species inhabits the Red Sea, grazing on algae on the lower shore.

PEARLY INSIDE
Abalones, or ear shells, are known for the beautiful, rainbow-sheen mother-of-pearl on the inside of the shell. These relatives of topshells and limpets graze on algae and are themselves eaten as a seafood delicacy, especially in western North America (where this species comes from) and the South Pacific.

Waste water is expelled through these holes

DEEP-DOWN SHINE
The serpent's-head cowrie is common around many shores of the Indian and Pacific Oceans, including all but the south coast of Australia. It crops small algae from the rocks and the outer edges of coral reefs, where the surf breaks. The animal withdraws into the slit on the shell's underside when in danger.

GATHERING SHELLFISH
Oysters have been gathered and eaten for many years. This Japanese woodcut print shows oyster fishermen at work near the sacred twin rocks off the island of Ise.

LIKE A PATTERNED TOY TOP
Monodonta is another boldly patterned topshell from the Indian Ocean. The topshells belong to the gastropod group of molluscs. Gastropod means "stomach-foot" and these animals, like their snail cousins, appear to slide along on their bellies.

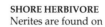

SHORE HERBIVORE
Nerites are found on many tropical coasts - these are from the Caribbean, where they live on the middle shore. These gastropods are herbivores (plant-eaters), scraping minute algae from rocks, roots, and large seaweeds.

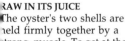

RAW IN ITS JUICE
The oyster's two shells are held firmly together by a strong muscle. To get at the flesh, the shells must be levered open with a knife. Oysters are often eaten raw in their natural juices, straight from the shell.

Spine for levering apart the plates of a barnacle

THE PREDATORY WHELK
Some dog whelks are snail-shaped, but the Chilean dog whelk is more limpet-like with a very large foot. It patrols the middle and lower shore of South America's Pacific coast, preying on barnacles and mussels.

FILTERING THE SEA
There are many species of oysters from different regions. This one, the rock oyster, cements itself to the rock, usually by its right-hand shell. Like many of its bivalve relatives, the oyster is a filter feeder. It draws in a current of seawater, filters out tiny floating food particles and passes these into its digestive system, using tiny beating hairs called cilia.

SHORE CARNIVORE
Dog whelks, like nerites (above), are gastropods, but unlike the nerites, they are carnivores (meat-eaters). This species, from North America's west coast, uses its spine to lever apart the plates of a barnacle and gain access to the flesh within.

MOLLUSC WITH DART
The Hebrew cone from the Indian and Pacific Oceans is an intertidal (p. 12) species belonging to the cone shells, a large group of gastropods. Cone shells have tiny poison "darts", harpoon-like structures that are fired into worms and other prey in order to subdue them.

WORM-HUNTING WHELK
The red-mouthed drupe is another type of dog whelk, named from the reddish "mouth" or opening of the shell. This species comes from the Indo-Pacific region, where it feeds on worms on the lower shore.

European cowries, smaller than their tropical counterparts, feed on sea-squirts on the lower shore

MUSSEL PROTECTION
Like its common edible relative, the green mussel attaches itself to rocks and pilings by tough threads called byssus. This species is found in Southeast Asia. Mussels are encouraged in some areas, since they are collected for food and bait.

SEA FOOD
In a clam-bake, depicted here by the 19th-century American artist Winslow Homer, the clams are cooked in a steaming bed of seaweed over hot stones.

Gripping the rock

ROCKY SEASHORES can be most unforgiving habitats, as waves pound unyielding stone. Many intertidal creatures have responded by evolving hard outer shells, which also protect them from predators and the sun's drying heat. Molluscs such as limpets have low, volcano-shaped shells that present little resistance to waves, while the periwinkle's shell is thick, tough, and rounded, so that if detached it is soon rolled to rest in a gulley. Another aid to survival is a good grip. Starfish and sea-urchins have hundreds of tiny "tube feet", while limpets and sea-snails have a single large suction "foot".

GRIPPING BY A STALK
Goose barnacles, which are often washed on to the shore, have tough stalks to grip any floating debris such as wood or pumice stone. These crustaceans (p. 44) live at sea, filtering tiny food particles from the water like their rock-bound shore relatives (p. 12). Once people believed that these barnacles hatched into geese - perhaps because their frilly limbs looked like feathers, or to explain the mysterious disappearance of the geese in winter.

Foot

Mouth

Chitons from above and below

Girdle

HELD BY SUCTION
The broad foot of the coat-of-mail shell, or chiton, anchors it to the shore. This mollusc can also clamp down its fleshy shell edge (girdle) to make a good seal and then raise its inner part to suck itself on to the rock. If dislodged, it flexes its body and rolls its jointed shell plates into a ball.

ANCHORED BY FEET
The five-rayed symmetry of the common sea-urchin indicates it is a cousin of starfish. It is protected from predators by formidable spines that can be tilted on ball-and-socket joints at their bases. It uses its long tube feet to anchor itself to the rock, drag itself along, seize bits of food or throw off debris.

Light-sensitive tentacle

Mouth

Foot

SEALING UP THE CRACKS
Edible or common periwinkles have long been gathered from the lower shore for food. Like its land relation, the snail, the periwinkle moves on a muscular, fleshy foot, lubricated by a film of mucus. When not "walking", it often nestles in a crack or gulley and seals the gap between its shell and the rock with mucus.

Sea-urchin's test

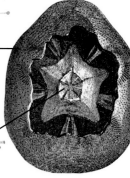

Holes where tube feet passed through

Mouth (Aristotle's lantern)

Anchoring tube feet

Tube feet searching water

Underside of common sea-urchin

THE INNER URCHIN
Without spines and skin, the beautifully patterned test (internal shell) of the sea-urchin is revealed. The system of five lever-operated teeth with which the urchin grazes seaweeds and encrusting animals is called Aristotle's lantern.

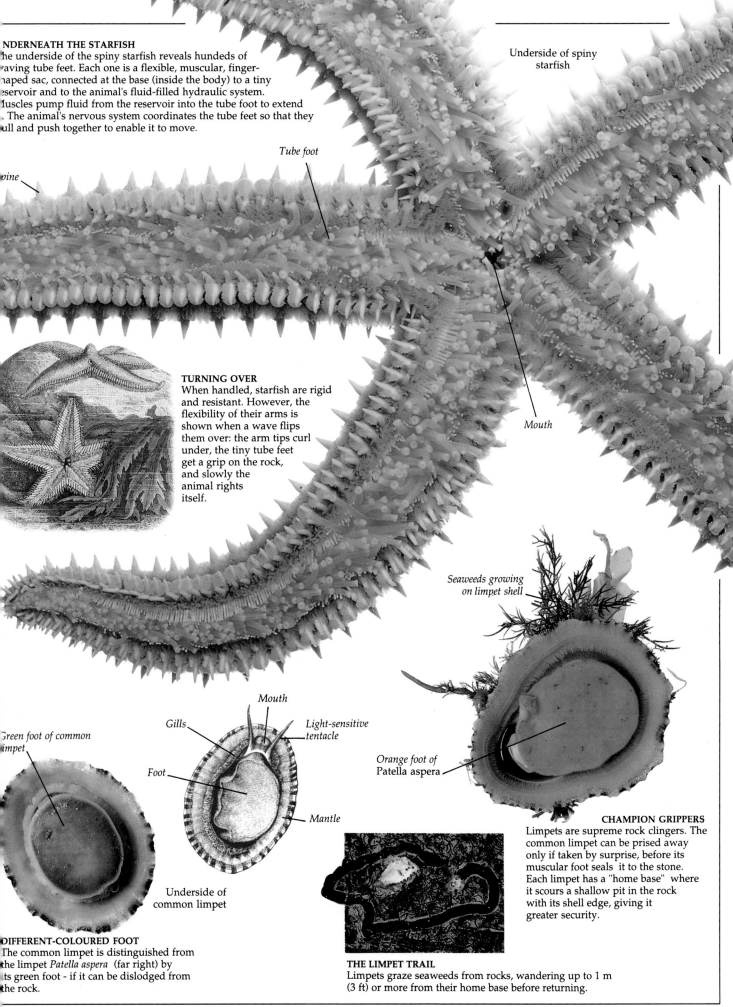

UNDERNEATH THE STARFISH

The underside of the spiny starfish reveals hundeds of waving tube feet. Each one is a flexible, muscular, finger-shaped sac, connected at the base (inside the body) to a tiny reservoir and to the animal's fluid-filled hydraulic system. Muscles pump fluid from the reservoir into the tube foot to extend it. The animal's nervous system coordinates the tube feet so that they pull and push together to enable it to move.

Spine

Tube foot

Underside of spiny starfish

Mouth

TURNING OVER

When handled, starfish are rigid and resistant. However, the flexibility of their arms is shown when a wave flips them over: the arm tips curl under, the tiny tube feet get a grip on the rock, and slowly the animal rights itself.

Seaweeds growing on limpet shell

Orange foot of Patella aspera

CHAMPION GRIPPERS

Limpets are supreme rock clingers. The common limpet can be prised away only if taken by surprise, before its muscular foot seals it to the stone. Each limpet has a "home base" where it scours a shallow pit in the rock with its shell edge, giving it greater security.

Green foot of common limpet

Mouth

Gills

Light-sensitive tentacle

Foot

Mantle

Underside of common limpet

DIFFERENT-COLOURED FOOT

The common limpet is distinguished from the limpet *Patella aspera* (far right) by its green foot - if it can be dislodged from the rock.

THE LIMPET TRAIL

Limpets graze seaweeds from rocks, wandering up to 1 m (3 ft) or more from their home base before returning.

Inside a rock pool

A ROCK POOL is a natural world in miniature - a specialized habitat in which plants and animals live together. A wide range of plants is found here, from the film of microscopic algae coating almost any bare surface, to wracks and other large seaweeds. These plants capture light energy from the sun and obtain nutrients from seawater. They provide food for winkles, limpets, and other plant-eaters. Flesh-eating animals such as starfish, small fish, whelks, and other creatures eat the plant-eaters. And then there are crabs, prawns, and other scavengers, that eat both plant and animal material. Water-sievers such as barnacles and mussels consume tiny particles of floating food, which may be miniature animals and plants, or bits of long-dead larger organisms.

STRINGS OF EGGS
Sea-hares come to the shore in spring and summer to browse on the seaweeds and lay their pinky-purple, string-like spawn.

NATURE STUDY
Naturalists have always been fascinated by rock pools. The great 19th-century English naturalist Philip Gosse studied shore life in Devon, southwest England. His son Edmund described how his father would "wade breast-high into one of the huge pools and examine the worm-eaten surface of the rock. . .there used often to lurk a marvellous profusion of animal and vegetable forms."

SLUGS OF THE SEA
Rock pools occasionally trap slug-like creatures such as this *Hypselodoris* from Guam, in the Pacific. They are called sea-slugs or nudibranchs, a name that means naked gills, after the feathery tufts on their backs which absorb oxygen from seawater. Sea-slugs (like land-slugs) are molluscs without shells.

TENTACLES LIKE A HARE'S EARS?
The sea-hare is not a true sea-slug since it has a thin, flexible shell hidden under the folds along its back.

RECYCLED STINGS
Some sea-slugs are equipped with stinging cells absorbed from anemones that they eat.

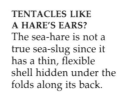

SPONGE EATER
The sea-lemon has a mottled yellowish body. It feeds on breadcrumb sponges (p. 19).

NOT RECOMMENDED
The bright colours of many sea-slugs warn potential predators that they taste horrible.

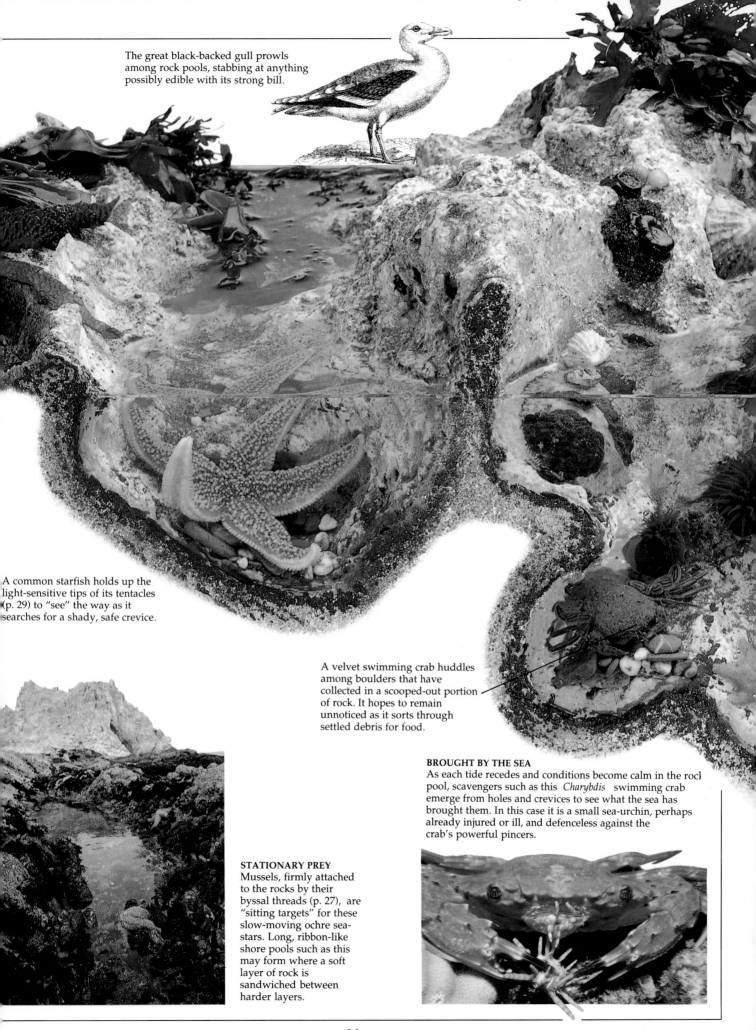

The great black-backed gull prowls among rock pools, stabbing at anything possibly edible with its strong bill.

A common starfish holds up the light-sensitive tips of its tentacles (p. 29) to "see" the way as it searches for a shady, safe crevice.

A velvet swimming crab huddles among boulders that have collected in a scooped-out portion of rock. It hopes to remain unnoticed as it sorts through settled debris for food.

BROUGHT BY THE SEA
As each tide recedes and conditions become calm in the rock pool, scavengers such as this *Charybdis* swimming crab emerge from holes and crevices to see what the sea has brought them. In this case it is a small sea-urchin, perhaps already injured or ill, and defenceless against the crab's powerful pincers.

STATIONARY PREY
Mussels, firmly attached to the rocks by their byssal threads (p. 27), are "sitting targets" for these slow-moving ochre sea-stars. Long, ribbon-like shore pools such as this may form where a soft layer of rock is sandwiched between harder layers.

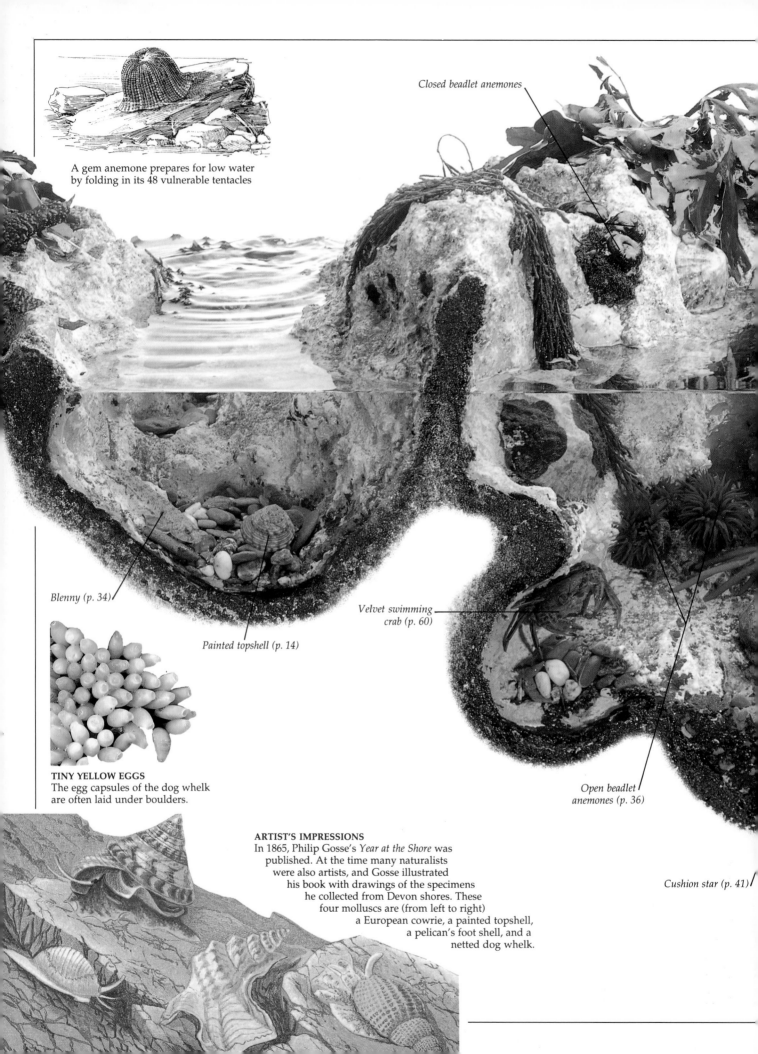

A gem anemone prepares for low water
by folding in its 48 vulnerable tentacles

Closed beadlet anemones

Blenny (p. 34)

Painted topshell (p. 14)

Velvet swimming
crab (p. 60)

TINY YELLOW EGGS
The egg capsules of the dog whelk
are often laid under boulders.

Open beadlet
anemones (p. 36)

Cushion star (p. 41)

ARTIST'S IMPRESSIONS
In 1865, Philip Gosse's *Year at the Shore* was
published. At the time many naturalists
were also artists, and Gosse illustrated
his book with drawings of the specimens
he collected from Devon shores. These
four molluscs are (from left to right)
a European cowrie, a painted topshell,
a pelican's foot shell, and a
netted dog whelk.

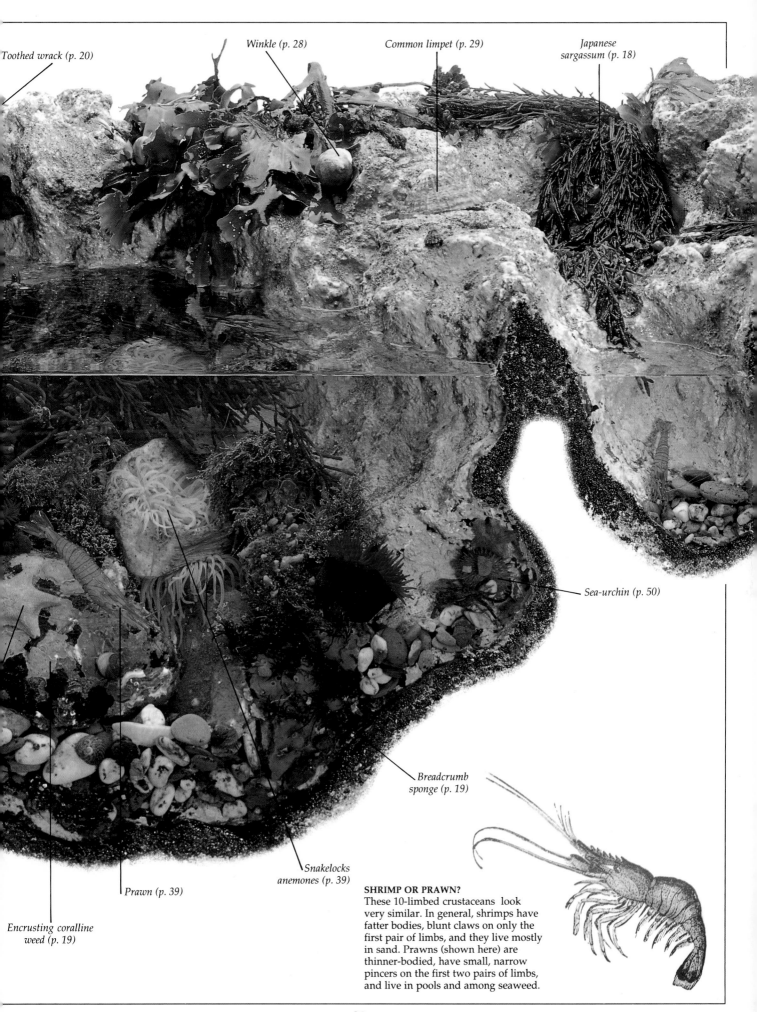

Toothed wrack (p. 20)

Winkle (p. 28)

Common limpet (p. 29)

Japanese sargassum (p. 18)

Sea-urchin (p. 50)

Breadcrumb sponge (p. 19)

Snakelocks anemones (p. 39)

Prawn (p. 39)

Encrusting coralline weed (p. 19)

SHRIMP OR PRAWN?
These 10-limbed crustaceans look very similar. In general, shrimps have fatter bodies, blunt claws on only the first pair of limbs, and they live mostly in sand. Prawns (shown here) are thinner-bodied, have small, narrow pincers on the first two pairs of limbs, and live in pools and among seaweed.

Rock-pool fish

LIFE FOR SMALL ANIMALS such as the tiny fish that live in rock pools is full of danger. If it rains heavily, the seawater in a small pool is greatly diluted, so that for a few hours the fish (and other inhabitants) must adjust their body chemistry to deal with the reduced concentration of salt. The falling tide may maroon them in a shallow puddle, so that they have to wriggle across bare rock to the safety of a deeper pool. In an hour, the sun can turn a cool pool into a warm bath, causing animals to leave the water and find refuge under a cool, moist rock rather than suffer a form of heatstroke. At low tide, gulls will feed on rock-pool inhabitants, before the returning tide brings waves that may roll boulders around which crush small creatures. Fishy predators are a constant threat: conger eels lurk in crevices, and hungry bass follow the tide in, snapping up any stragglers. The fish shown here have to be hardy creatures to survive the fluctuating conditions and physical threats in the miniature habitat of the rock pool.

A FLICK OF THE FINS
There are about 1,500 species in the goby family, most of them small, flattened, tough-looking shore dwellers. These are sand gobies, which can immerse themselves in sand with a flick of the fins.

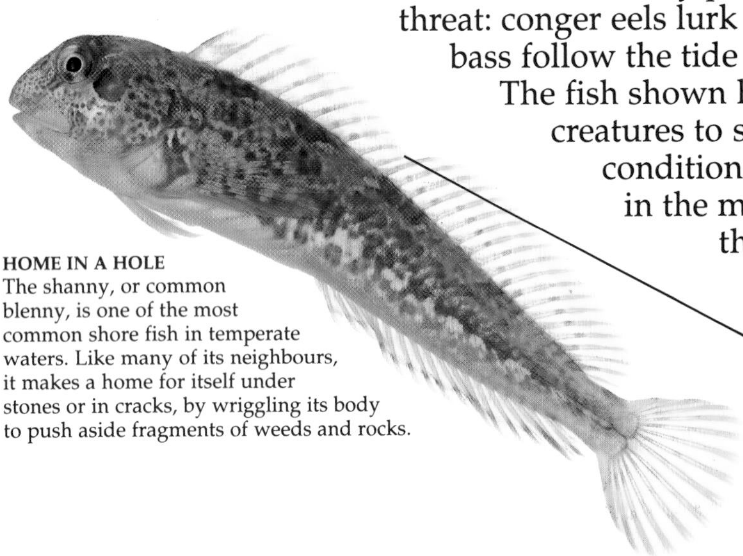

DANGER AFOOT
Many shore fish are so well camouflaged that they are unseen by walkers on the shore, and must dart away from a descending boot.

HOME IN A HOLE
The shanny, or common blenny, is one of the most common shore fish in temperate waters. Like many of its neighbours, it makes a home for itself under stones or in cracks, by wriggling its body to push aside fragments of weeds and rocks.

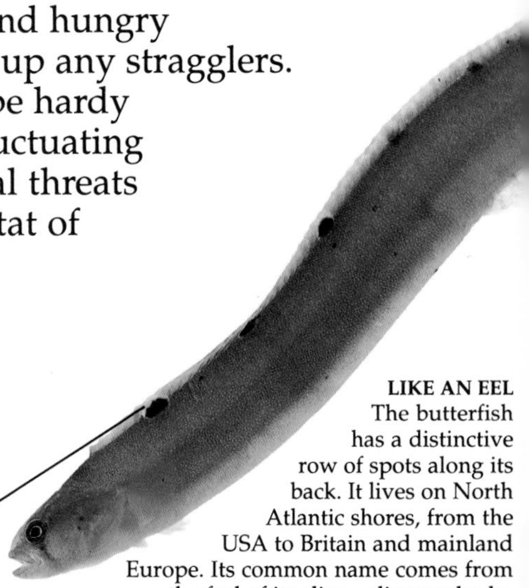

Distinctive dip in the middle of the dorsal (back) fin

Dark spots along the base of the dorsal fin

LIKE AN EEL
The butterfish has a distinctive row of spots along its back. It lives on North Atlantic shores, from the USA to Britain and mainland Europe. Its common name comes from the feel of its slimy, slippery body.

LOOKING UPWARDS
Shore fish have eyes that are closer to the tops of their heads than many other fish. This enables them to watch for predators from above, such as seabirds.

Shanny

Butterfish

Blenny

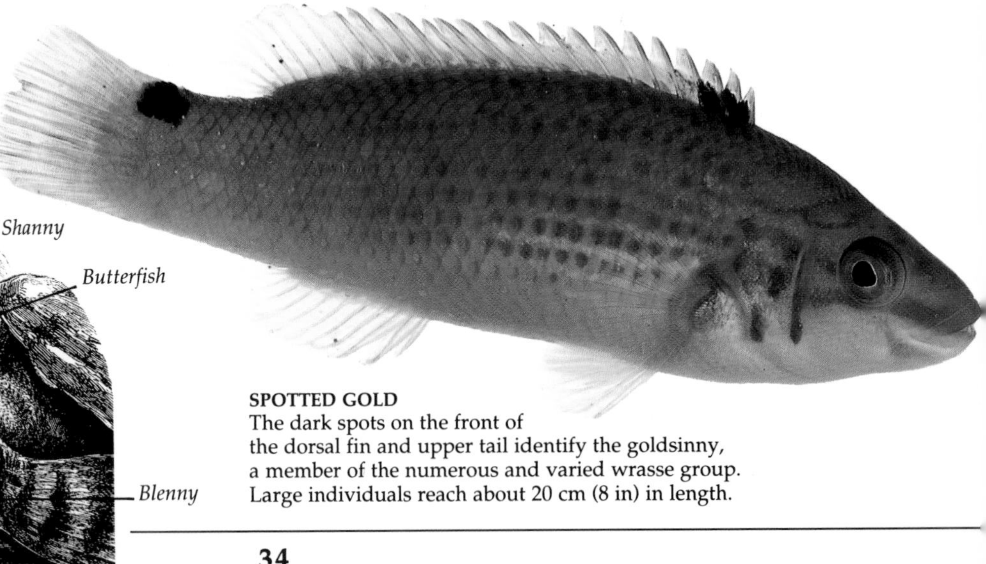

SPOTTED GOLD
The dark spots on the front of the dorsal fin and upper tail identify the goldsinny, a member of the numerous and varied wrasse group. Large individuals reach about 20 cm (8 in) in length.

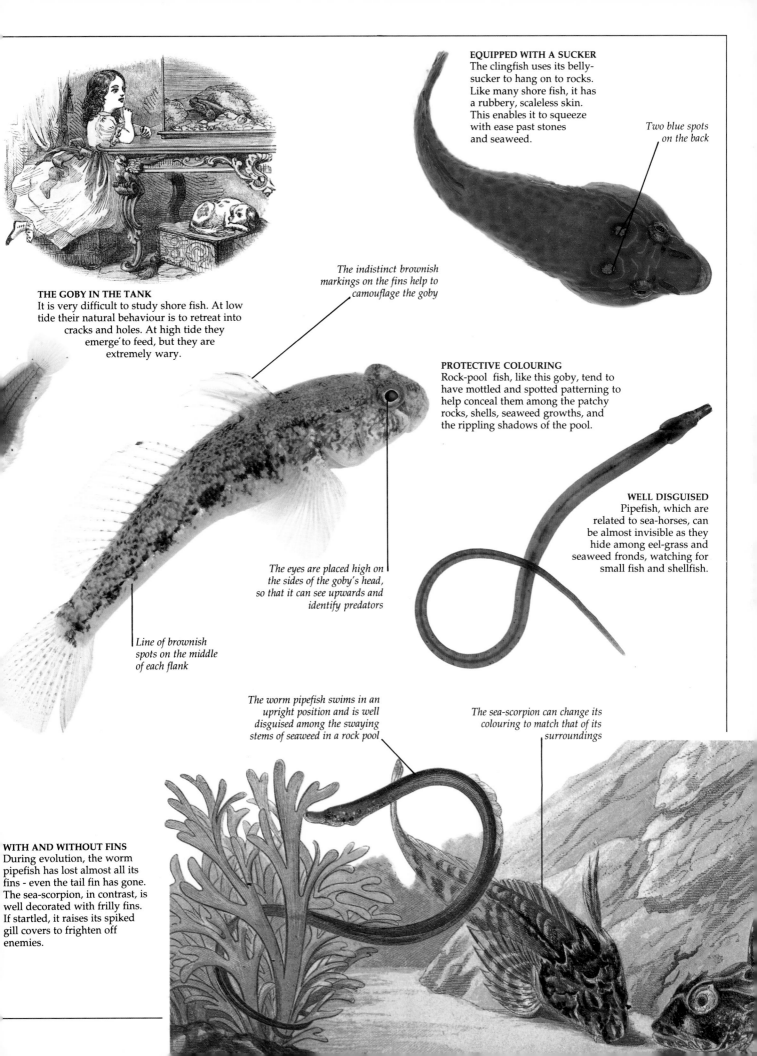

EQUIPPED WITH A SUCKER
The clingfish uses its belly-sucker to hang on to rocks. Like many shore fish, it has a rubbery, scaleless skin. This enables it to squeeze with ease past stones and seaweed.

Two blue spots on the back

The indistinct brownish markings on the fins help to camouflage the goby

THE GOBY IN THE TANK
It is very difficult to study shore fish. At low tide their natural behaviour is to retreat into cracks and holes. At high tide they emerge to feed, but they are extremely wary.

PROTECTIVE COLOURING
Rock-pool fish, like this goby, tend to have mottled and spotted patterning to help conceal them among the patchy rocks, shells, seaweed growths, and the rippling shadows of the pool.

The eyes are placed high on the sides of the goby's head, so that it can see upwards and identify predators

WELL DISGUISED
Pipefish, which are related to sea-horses, can be almost invisible as they hide among eel-grass and seaweed fronds, watching for small fish and shellfish.

Line of brownish spots on the middle of each flank

The worm pipefish swims in an upright position and is well disguised among the swaying stems of seaweed in a rock pool

The sea-scorpion can change its colouring to match that of its surroundings

WITH AND WITHOUT FINS
During evolution, the worm pipefish has lost almost all its fins - even the tail fin has gone. The sea-scorpion, in contrast, is well decorated with frilly fins. If startled, it raises its spiked gill covers to frighten off enemies.

Flower-like animals

OPEN FOR DINNER
Beautiful but deadly:
the waving tentacles of
an anemone colony are a
forest of danger for small
sea creatures.

Scallop shell

ANEMONES are the surprising "flowers" of the shore
- surprising because they are not flowers at all. They
are hollow, jelly-like animals belonging to a group
called the coelenterates or cnidarians, which also
includes jellyfish and corals. Their "petals" are
tentacles equipped with specialized stinging cells
that poison prey, which is pulled inwards to the
mouth (p. 39). Like flowers, anemones have
evolved many beautiful colours, from salmon
pink to emerald green and jet black. In many
there is great colour variation, even within the
same species. Another remarkable feature is the
fact that many can move, if only slowly, sliding
their muscular bases along the rock surface.
Certain species burrow in sand and gravel, while
others slide their bodies into crevices in the rocks so
that only their tentacles show. As the
tide ebbs, most anemones on
the shore pull in their
tentacles and become
jelly-like blobs, to
avoid drying out.

*Mouth in centre
of body*

SWEEPING THE SEA
Fan worms are sometimes
mistaken for anemones, but they
belong to a different group of
animals - the annelids (which
include earthworms). The tentacles
of the "fan" filter tiny food particles
from the water and withdraw in a
flash into the tube if danger
threatens.

TRAFFIC-LIGHT ANEMONES
Beadlet anemones come in
various colours, including red,
amber, and green. When the tide
recedes, they fold in their tentacles,
looking like overgrown wine-gums
scattered on the rocks. When
fully grown they have
about 200 tentacles.

**BLEMISH
OR BEAUTY?**
The wart-like knobs on
this creature's body
have led to one of its
common names -
wartlet
anemone.
The
warts can
be seen on
the closed
wartlet
anemone
on the
page
opposite.

*Calcareous (chalky) algae
encrusting rock*

"FLOWER" ON A "STALK"
This side view of a greyish
beadlet anemone shows its stubby "stalk"
(body) with an iridescent sheen around the
base. Beadlets can survive being out of water
for some time and can live quite high on the shore.

FEATHERY PLUMES
The plumose or frilled
anemone is brown, reddish,
or white and may grow up to 30 cm (1 ft)
tall. Its feathery tentacles catch very small
bits of food and waft them down to the mouth
by the beating action of tiny hairs called cilia.

Snow-white tentacles and brown body of a beadlet anemone

Living cup coral with tentacles extended

Limy skeleton of dead cup coral

PINK-TIPPED TENTACLES
Snakelocks anemones range from grey with delicate sheens of pink or green to all-over deep green. The tentacles, tipped in deep pink, do not withdraw in this species, even when it is out of water.

LIVING CORAL
Corals are similar to anemones and members of the same group, the coelenterates (cnidarians). This cup coral lives alone, unlike its tropical reef-building cousins.

Side view of dead cup coral

The body "warts" of this wartlet anemone are visible in this closed-up individual

GIANT OF ITS KIND
The largest anemones may grow to more than 1 m (3 ft) across. This is a giant green anemone from tropical waters.

Strings (acontia) of stinging cells

TINY GHOSTS
There are many different species of these tiny, ghost-white encrusting anemones covering some areas of rocky shore.

STINGING STRINGS
The colourful sagartia anemone (this is the "rosea" variety) is one of several species that eject pale stringy groups of stinging cells through its mouth or through slits in its body to defend itself or to catch a meal. The "strings" are in fact parts of the animal's guts!

MINIATURE FANS
Fan worms (see opposite page) live inside protective, chalky tubes. Some species live buried in the mud, others attach themselves to rocks, as here. Look to the left - can you spot another small fan worm on the opposite corner of this stone?

Encrusted remains of barnacle shells

Coiled, chalky remains of tube worm

Tentacles and stings

THE COELENTERATE (CNIDARIAN) ANIMALS (jellyfish, anemones, and corals) are the stingers of the shore. These creatures do not have brains or sophisticated sense organs such as eyes and ears. They are unable to move quickly, so they cannot escape from predators or pursue prey. For them, the best form of defence and attack lies in the tiny stinging cells contained in their tentacles. Inside each cell is a capsule called a nematocyst, which contains a long, coiled thread. In some species these are barbed, in others they contain venom. Stimulated by touch or by certain chemicals, the threads flick out and then either the barbs hold on to the prey, or venom is injected into it. Then the animal drags its victim into the digestive cavity within the body. Some jellyfish have exceedingly powerful venom that can cause great pain if bathers brush against them, and their nematocysts remain active for a time even after the animal is washed up and dies on the shore. The best known is the Portuguese man-of-war "jellyfish". This is not a true jellyfish, but a colony of small animals from the same group. A swimmer may be stung without ever seeing the creature responsible, since the tentacles trail in the current several metres (yards) behind the floating body. The box jellyfish, or sea-wasp, of tropical waters has tentacles up to 10 m (33 ft) long and its stings are lethal to humans.

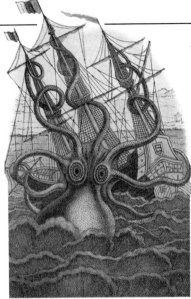

KRAKEN AHOY
The Kraken, a sea monster of Norse legend, made short work of ships and their crews. As is often the case, the fable has some basis in fact. The Kraken bears more than a passing resemblance to the squid, a member of the mollusc group. Atlantic giant squid have been recorded at 15 m (50 ft) long, including tentacles, and 2 tonnes (tons) in weight, and their remains are sometimes washed up on the shore (p. 56).

Common prawn

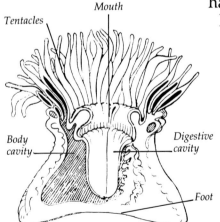

Mouth

Tentacles

Body cavity

Digestive cavity

Foot

INSIDE AN ANEMONE
Anemones, and their coelenterate (cnidarian) relatives, are simply constructed creatures. The ring of tentacles surrounds a mouth which leads to the digestive cavity inside the body. Prey is pushed into the cavity, digested, and absorbed, and any remains excreted through the mouth.

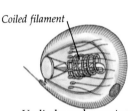

Coiled filament

Discharged filament

Undischarged nematocyst   Discharged nematocyst

THE STINGING THREAD
Under the microscope it is possible to see tiny sting-containing cells on the tentacles of coelenterate (cnidarian) animals. When the cell is triggered by touch or certain chemicals, its internal fluid pressure quickly increases. This forces the thread-like filament to shoot out. Some filaments are barbed; others contain venom.

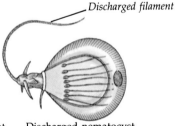

PRAWN SNACK
This snakelocks anemone is in the process of capturing a common prawn and pulling it towards its mouth. The barbed stinging cells in the tentacles help to subdue the prey and paralyze it. When the prawn is drawn into the anemone's stomach, more stings will finish it off.

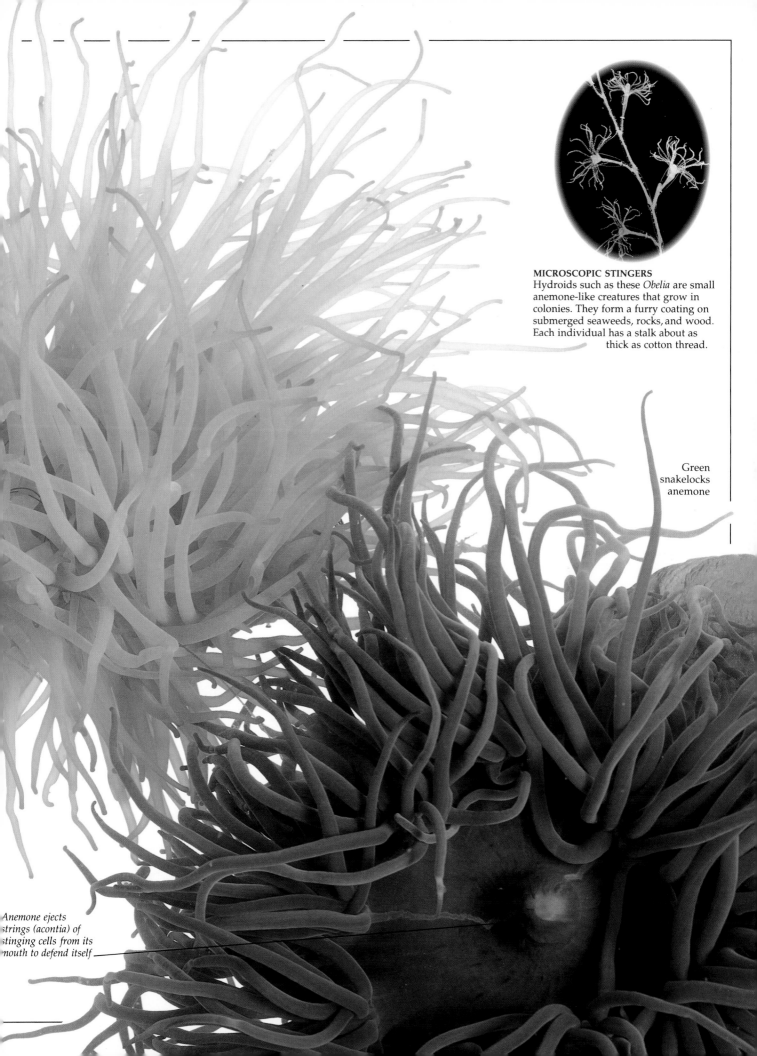

MICROSCOPIC STINGERS
Hydroids such as these *Obelia* are small
anemone-like creatures that grow in
colonies. They form a furry coating on
submerged seaweeds, rocks, and wood.
Each individual has a stalk about as
thick as cotton thread.

Green
snakelocks
anemone

Anemone ejects
strings (acontia) of
stinging cells from its
mouth to defend itself

Stars of the sea

IN THE LIMELIGHT
Sunbeams shining through the surface of a rock pool spotlight shore starfish. The "sausage-with-a-frill" (upper right) is a sea-cucumber. In this relative of the starfish, the arms are tentacles around the mouth end.

On almost any seashore, somewhere, there will be starfish - and probably a few of their relatives such as the brittlestars, sea-urchins, and sea-cucumbers. These creatures belong to a group called the echinoderms (meaning "spiny skinned") and they have been around for perhaps 500 million years. Starfish that are not spiny are protected by an outer skeleton (exoskeleton) of hard, limy plates embedded just under the tough skin. Although there are more than 6,000 species of echinoderms - 2,000 more species than there are within the mammal group - these creatures are sea-dwellers, so they are unfamiliar to most people. They also seem strange because their body plan consists of "arms" arranged like rays coming from a central point. There is no front end: when a starfish goes for a walk, to follow the retreating tide or find a cool spot out of the sun, any arm can take the lead.

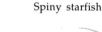
Light-sensitive tips of arms often turn up to "see" the way

Spiny starfish

A THORNY PROBLEM
The crown-of-thorns starfish feeds on coral. From time to time its numbers increase dramatically, causing much damage in places such as Australia's Great Barrier Reef. Whether this is a natural cycle, or the result of pollution, is not clear.

NEWLY ARMED
Starfish can grow new arms. If an arm is crushed by a waveswept boulder or mauled by a predator, it can be cast off and a new one grows. In fact, provided most of the central disc is intact, one remaining arm can grow four new ones.

Brittlestar

SNAKING MOVEMENT
The brittlestar throws its fragile arms into serpent-like shapes as it glides swiftly through a shore pool. The arms really are brittle and easily broken, but the brittlestar is able to grow new ones.

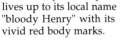
Scarlet starfish

SEEING RED
The scarlet starfish, seen occasionally on rocky shores, lives up to its local name "bloody Henry" with its vivid red body marks.

MUSSEL POWER
The common starfish preys on molluscs such as mussels. It wraps itself around the victim, grips with its "tube feet", gradually pulls open the two shells, and protrudes its stomach to digest the prey's soft parts.

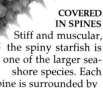
COVERED IN SPINES
Stiff and muscular, the spiny starfish is one of the larger sea-shore species. Each calcareous (chalky) spine is surrounded by tiny pincer-like organs (pedicellariae). It uses these to rid itself of parasites, small hitch-hikers, and other debris. This starfish feeds on bivalve molluscs.

Common
starfish

LEFT STRANDED
Most starfish live low on the shore or in deeper
water. Those washed up by heavy seas and
stranded out of the water may not survive until
the tide returns.

COMMONLY ORANGE
Many common starfish are
orange, but some are brown,
red, or even purple.
Colour variation is
frequent among
these creatures.

HUNGRY STARLETS
Small cushion stars, or "starlets", are no less
carnivorous (meat-eating) than their larger
cousins, devouring little molluscs,
brittlestars, and
shore worms.

Goosefoot starfish (right)

Common
sunstar
(below)

WEBBED ARMS
Although the goosefoot starfish
(far right) looks like a five-sided
sticking plaster, it is an active predator
and feeds on crustaceans, molluscs,
and other starfish.

TWELVE-RAYED SUN
This common sunstar (right) has
12 arms, but individuals with as few
as eight or as many as 13 are not
unusual. Like the goosefoot
starfish, it will eat other
echinoderms such as
the common starfish.

Borers and builders

O<small>N THE COAST OF CALIFORNIA</small> in the late 1920s, steel girders and piles were installed for a seaside pier. About 20 years later, the 1 cm (.4 in) thick steel was honey combed with holes. The culprit was the North American purple urchin. This animal, like many others on the shore, takes refuge from waves, predators, sunshine, and cold by boring into the substance of the shore itself. Sand and mud, being easier to move than solid rock, contain many burrowers, such as razorshells, cockles, gapers, clams, and tellins. (A razorshell is reputed to burrow as fast as a human can dig down after it.) Yet even on a rocky shore there are burrowers, boring, scraping, and dissolving their way into the rock. They include the piddock which, as it wears away the surface layer of its shell by drilling, moves the fleshy part of its body over the worn shell and lays down a fresh layer of a hard, chalky substance. Pieces of wood riddled with long holes some 2 cm (.8 in) across are often cast up on the beach. These are the work of shipworms, which despite their appearance are not worms but bivalve molluscs (p. 26), like piddocks.

HIDEY-HOLES IN THE ROCK
Rock-boring sea-urchins have made many holes in this section of limestone coast at The Burren, southwest Ireland. Unoccupied holes collect pebbles that are swirled around by the sea, scouring the rock still further. In these ways, rock-boring urchins and molluscs contribute to the erosion of the shore.

Date mussels in limestone

DISSOLVING STONE
The date mussel of the Mediterranean is one of sever molluscs that can insert itself into solid rock. Here two sma specimens have bored into limestone, while on the large individual (left) the growth rings typical of many bivalve molluscs are visible. The mussel gives off chemicals, which eat their way into the rock, rather than using physical abrasion like the piddock. Its scientific name is *Lithophaga*, which means "eating rock".

Growth ring

BUILDING A HOME
Several kinds of marine worms make tubes around themselves, chiefly to protect their soft bodies. *Terebella* (left) manipulates tiny particles with its tentacles and glues them together with a sticky body secretion. *Serpula* (centre) makes a chalky, trumpet-shaped tube. Fan worms (right) make tubes that protrude above lower-shore sand.

TRIANGLE TUBES
Keelworms are another type of tube-building marine worm. Their chalky tubes have a "keel" or edge, so that they appear triangular in cross-section. Their feathery tentacles collect tiny bits of food from seawater.

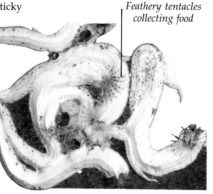

Feathery tentacles collecting food

Piddock in mudstone

PRISONER IN SOLID ROCK
The piddock's shell bears a passing resemblance to the sharply ribbed drilling bit of an oil rig, and not without reason. This mollusc twists and rocks the two parts (valves) of its shell in order to drill itself a hole in solid rock. Two long, fleshy tubes, called siphons, reach up the hole and extend beyond it. Seawater is sucked down one tube to supply the animal with oxygen and food, while waste and rock debris are passed out of the other siphon

...ROW IN A BURROW

...veral species of sea-urchin are able to make ...allow depressions in the rock, and some ...n burrow almost out of sight. The rock-...ring or purple burrowing sea-urchin ...oves its strong, stout spines to and ...n and gradually rasps its way into ...e rock. It also grinds away the ...ck with its gnawing mouth-...rts. As it grows and burrows, ...may be unable to escape from ...tunnel and become ...pendent on capturing food ...th its tube feet (p. 28).

Skeleton (test)

Urchins shelter in shallow "caves" excavated in rock

Spines are purple in life

...OCK RESIDENT

...he North American purple urchin lives on the lower ...ore and in the shallows. Above the low-tide mark, ...scrapes a shallow "home" in the rock.

Holes where sponge's breathing and feeding pores are exposed (p. 19)

Borings of yellow sponge

...hell of flat oyster

A BORING ANIMAL

The yellow boring sponge makes branching tunnels in limestone or the chalky substance of a thick sea shell, by dissolving the minerals with an acidic substance. Small parts of the sponge project above each tunnel, bearing either one large hole (pore) which waste water passes out of, or several smaller sieve-covered holes through which water is drawn in (p. 19).

Hard cases

SOME OF THE MOST CURIOUS-LOOKING creatures of the shore are crabs, prawns, and lobsters. They are members of a large and varied group of animals called the crustaceans. In the same way that insects swarm on land, so crustaceans teem in the sea. Both groups are arthropods or joint-legged animals. Crustaceans usually have jointed limbs (up to 17 pairs in some species), two pairs of antennae, and a hard shell, or carapace, that encloses and protects much of the body. However, the animals themselves vary enormously. They range from microscopic creatures that make up a large part of the floating plankton (the "soup" that nourishes so many filter-feeding sea animals), to the giant spider crabs of Japan, which measure more than 3.5 m (12 ft) across the claw-tips. Some of the most surprising members of the crustacean group are the barnacles (cirripeds). These animals begin life as tiny, free-swimming larvae. Some species then settle on the shore, cement their heads to the rock, grow hard plates around their bodies, and use their six pairs of feathery, jointed "legs" to kick food into their mouths! The crustaceans most familiar to us are the decapods, which include shore creatures such as crabs, lobsters, crawfish, hermit crabs, prawns, and shrimps. Decapod means "10-legged", and most of these creatures have 10 main limbs. Four pairs are for walking or swimming, and there is one pair of manipulating pincers.

POTTED CRAB
Crabs have long been caught, cooked, and eaten by people. Crab pots are filled with rotting flesh as bait; once the crab has entered, it is unable to climb out. Crabs are also eaten by shore birds and mammals, by fish such as bass, and by octopuses.

The pugnacious shore crab, pincers held up in self-defence, is known in France as *le crabe enragé*

BATTLE-SCARRED SCUTTLER
This shore crab has lost one of its limbs. A herring gull's powerful bill, or perhaps a small rock rolled by a wave, has removed its right first walking leg. Accidents like this often happen to crabs on rocky shores. However this individual is not disabled by this loss and displays a variety of postures, from caution (below) to mock attack, then a crouching defence, and next a backwards right-angled turn to allow finally a retreat.

THE RED CARPET
In some areas of the Galapagos islands off the coast of Ecuador, Sally Lightfoot crabs cover surf-splashed rocks like a moving red carpet. This brilliantly coloured species has bright red limbs and a sky-blue underside.

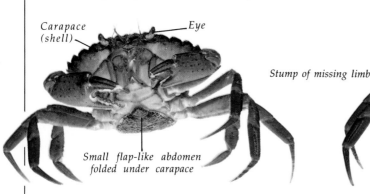

Carapace (shell)   *Eye*

Small flap-like abdomen folded under carapace

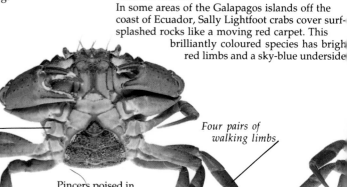

Stump of missing limb

Four pairs of walking limbs

Pincers poised in mock attack

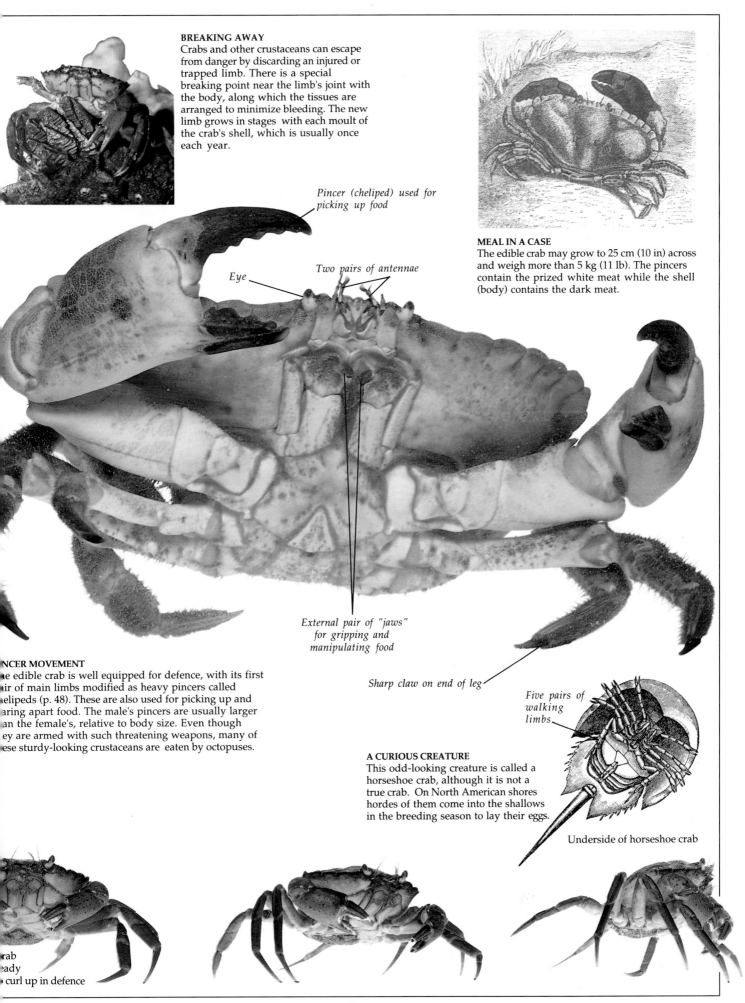

BREAKING AWAY
Crabs and other crustaceans can escape
from danger by discarding an injured or
trapped limb. There is a special
breaking point near the limb's joint with
the body, along which the tissues are
arranged to minimize bleeding. The new
limb grows in stages with each moult of
the crab's shell, which is usually once
each year.

*Pincer (cheliped) used for
picking up food*

Eye

Two pairs of antennae

MEAL IN A CASE
The edible crab may grow to 25 cm (10 in) across
and weigh more than 5 kg (11 lb). The pincers
contain the prized white meat while the shell
(body) contains the dark meat.

*External pair of "jaws"
for gripping and
manipulating food*

PINCER MOVEMENT
The edible crab is well equipped for defence, with its first
pair of main limbs modified as heavy pincers called
chelipeds (p. 48). These are also used for picking up and
tearing apart food. The male's pincers are usually larger
than the female's, relative to body size. Even though
they are armed with such threatening weapons, many of
these sturdy-looking crustaceans are eaten by octopuses.

Sharp claw on end of leg

*Five pairs of
walking
limbs*

A CURIOUS CREATURE
This odd-looking creature is called a
horseshoe crab, although it is not a
true crab. On North American shores
hordes of them come into the shallows
in the breeding season to lay their eggs.

Underside of horseshoe crab

crab
ready
curl up in defence

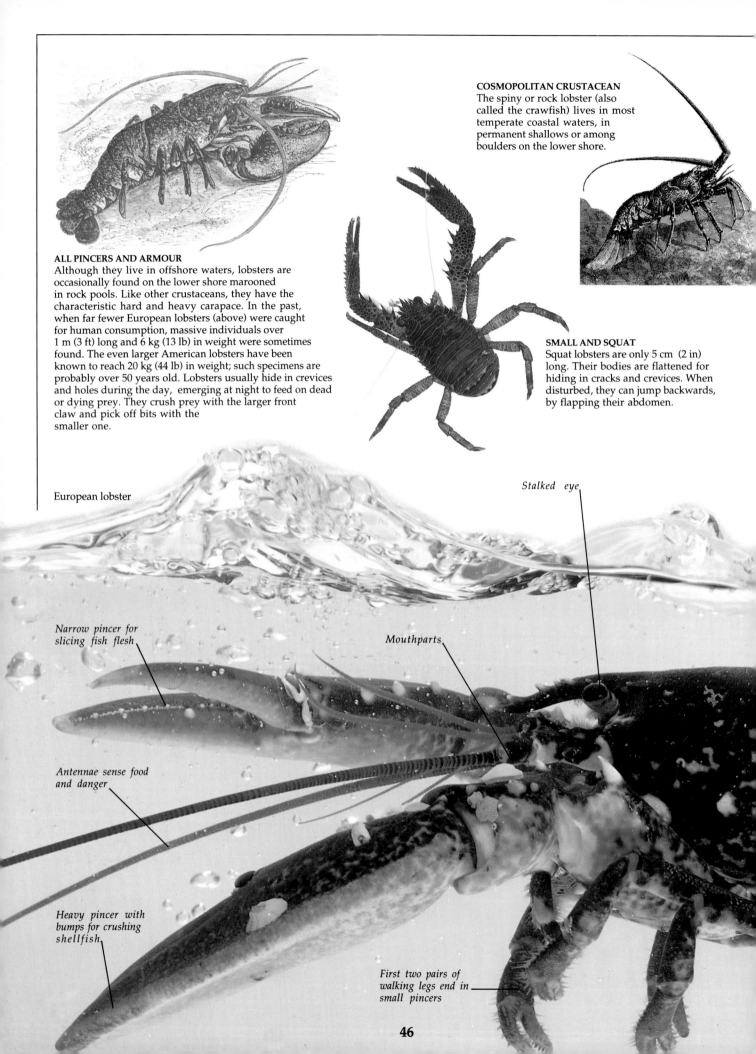

COSMOPOLITAN CRUSTACEAN
The spiny or rock lobster (also called the crawfish) lives in most temperate coastal waters, in permanent shallows or among boulders on the lower shore.

ALL PINCERS AND ARMOUR
Although they live in offshore waters, lobsters are occasionally found on the lower shore marooned in rock pools. Like other crustaceans, they have the characteristic hard and heavy carapace. In the past, when far fewer European lobsters (above) were caught for human consumption, massive individuals over 1 m (3 ft) long and 6 kg (13 lb) in weight were sometimes found. The even larger American lobsters have been known to reach 20 kg (44 lb) in weight; such specimens are probably over 50 years old. Lobsters usually hide in crevices and holes during the day, emerging at night to feed on dead or dying prey. They crush prey with the larger front claw and pick off bits with the smaller one.

SMALL AND SQUAT
Squat lobsters are only 5 cm (2 in) long. Their bodies are flattened for hiding in cracks and crevices. When disturbed, they can jump backwards, by flapping their abdomen.

European lobster

Stalked eye

Narrow pincer for slicing fish flesh

Mouthparts

Antennae sense food and danger

Heavy pincer with bumps for crushing shellfish

First two pairs of walking legs end in small pincers

46

NOT ONLY ROCK-BOTTOM

The coral crab lives in various habitats, frequenting rocky-bottomed shores, sandy areas, and sponges on coral reefs. It is found along the east coast of North America.

CRAB IN THE SKY

Early astronomers saw a crab-like pattern of stars in the northern night sky, and named it Cancer after the Latin word for a crab. Cancer is also the fourth sign of the zodiac, with the Sun passing through from about 21 June to 22 July.

A CLEANER COAST

Most crabs are adept scavengers, and the furrowed crab is no exception, picking up almost anything edible from the sea-bed. It lives around European coasts.

Barnacle cemented to lobster's body

Growth of sea-mats, a colony of tiny anemone-like animals (p. 25)

Tail-fan helps to propel lobster backwards when the tail is straightened and then suddenly flexed

Tail (abdomen)

econd two pairs of alking legs end in aws

Curly, protective tube of small marine worm

Swimmerets under tail enable lobster to bounce and swim as it moves along the bottom

47

Unusual partnerships

THERE ARE MANY TYPES of relationships in the animal world. A very familiar example is when one animal hunts and eats another. This is the predator-prey relationship. Yet nature is not always so cut and thrust. On the seashore, as in other habitats, different kinds of animals are regularly seen together. This does not happen by chance - there is a reason. Scientists have different names for these relationships. In the relationship that is called parasitism, one partner, the parasite, gains, but the other, the host, loses. Some shore crabs are host to *Sacculina*, a strange creature related to the barnacles. *Sacculina* attaches itself to a young crab and then grows "tentacles" that eat into the crab's body, thus gaining nourishment and disabling the crab. Another type of relationship, in which both part-ners benefit, is called symbiosis. The hermit crab and the calliactis anemone live in this way. The calliactis is sometimes called the parasitic anemone, but it does not seem to harm its hermit host. It feeds on particles that the crab drops, while the crab is protected by the stinging tentacles.

HERMITS AT HOME
Hermit crabs do not have shells of their own, so they have to look for shells of dead animals to hide their soft bodies in. Often, when they move to larger shells as they grow, they carefully remove any anemones from the old shell and "plant" them on the new one. There are also land hermit crabs in the tropics. Some species live in hollow mangrove roots or bamboo stems.

THREE-IN-ONE
Each of the three animals in this "partnership" comes from a different major animal group. The hermit crab is a crustacean (p. 44). The anemone is a coelenterate (cnidarian) (p. 36). The shell once belonged to a whelk, which is a sea-snail and member of the mollusc group (p. 26).

STING IN THE PINCER
The boxer crab carries small anemones in its pincers. They act as "stinging clubs" and are waved at any creature posing a threat.

Keelworm tube inside shell

CLAW IN THE DOOR
In its defensive position, the hermit crab pulls itself deep inside the shell. The right front claw (cheliped), which bears the large pincer, is usually bigger than the left one, and the crab holds it across the shell's entrance to make an effect-ive door. (In this example the pincer is missing; it may have been bitten off by a predator or squashed by a boulder.)

SWEEPING THE FLOOR
The tentacles of anemones reach upwards for floating or swimming victims. A calliactis anemone on a hermit crab's shell tends to hang down and sweep the rocks for bits of food "spilt" by the hermit crab.

Small closed anemone

Whelk shell

Soft abdomen

Main claw for closing shell entrance

Back legs

OUT OF ITS SHELL
The hermit crab's soft, curled abdomen is clearly visible when the animal comes out of its shell. When it grows too big for the shell, it looks for another, larger shell. The two back pairs of legs are small and adapted for hanging on to the inside of the shell.

Main claw (cheliped) missing

Long antenna

Tentacles search the water for food

ON THE MOVE
When the hermit crab is moving about, its head, antennae (feelers), front claws, and first two pairs of legs are exposed. Like its crab cousins, the hermit crab is a scavenger and feeds on bits of dead and dying animals, and plants - in fact on almost anything edible. A dying animal on the shore is soon surrounded by a horde of crabs, picking and pulling at the flesh.

SAFE AMONG THE STINGS
Clown fish (these are tomato clowns) live among the stinging tentacles of anemones. The fish have special defences in their body coverings to prevent them from being stung. It is believed that both partners benefit from this arrangement, in various ways. The clown fish are safe in the protective tentacles; they may drive off other fish that nibble at the anemone; and they may eat leftover food caught by the anemone. The anemone may be "cleaned" in the process and it may eat food dropped by the clown fish. It is also possible that the brightly coloured clown fish attract predators, which the anemone then seizes.

HOME IN A CONE
Not all hermit crabs live in whelk shells. This Pacific flat hermit crab is occupying an empty omaria cone shell. The cone shells are tropical molluscs; some species are extremely venomous.

Disguises

A CASUAL GLANCE into a rock pool may reveal only a few strands of seaweed and some dead-looking shells. But wait patiently, sitting low and still to avoid being seen, and watch carefully. A dark patch of rock may suddenly glide forward: it is a blenny, on the look-out for food. A slightly hazy-looking area of sand walks away: it is a prawn, adjusting the spots and lines on its body to blend perfectly with the background. A small pebble slides off: it is a winkle grazing on algae. A patch of gravelly bottom ripples, and two eyes appear: a flatfish has wafted small pebbles and shell fragments over its body to break up its outline. All these creatures use camouflage to help conceal themselves. Looks are not everything, though - behaviour is important too. The eel-like pipefish (p. 34) tends to swim in an upright position, to merge in with the ribbons of seaweed and eel-grass in which it hides.

PALE UNDERSIDE
Flatfish are usually well camouflaged when viewed from the surface of the water. The underside, flat against the sea-bed, has no need of special colouring, so it is white or pale in many species.

LOOKING LIKE A WEED
The leafy sea-dragon, from the coastal waters of southern Australia, is a a type of sea-horse. Its loose lobes of skin resemble the seaweed fronds in which it hides.

URCHIN COVER UP
Several species of sea-urchins grasp pebbles, shells, and pieces of seaweed with their long "tube feet" (p. 28) and hold them over their bodies. A well-draped urchin can be difficult to spot. These are green sea-urchins, which are found on the lower shore and inshore waters.

DAB HAND AT CHANGE
Many flatfish can change their colouring to match the bottom on which they are resting. Some minutes earlier this young dab was a light sandy colour. I soon became several shades darker when placed on selected dark pebbles. The marks on its upper side became almost black. The largest dabs reach about 40 cm (16 in) long

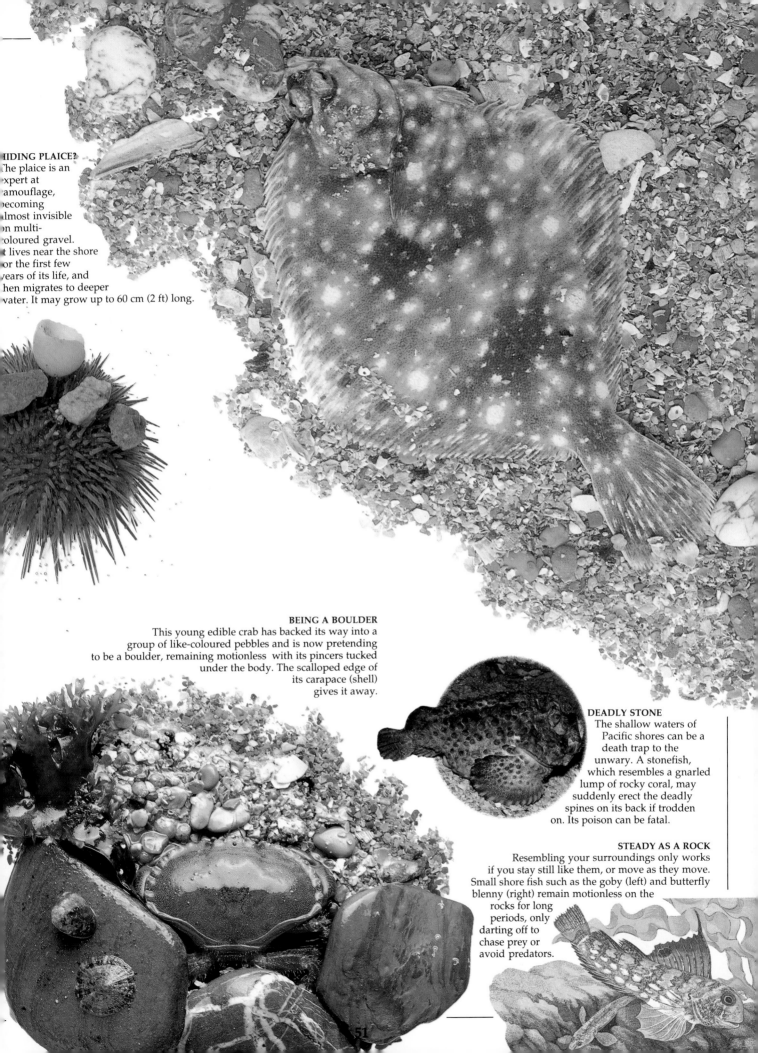

HIDING PLAICE?
The plaice is an
expert at
camouflage,
becoming
almost invisible
on multi-
coloured gravel.
It lives near the shore
for the first few
years of its life, and
then migrates to deeper
water. It may grow up to 60 cm (2 ft) long.

BEING A BOULDER
This young edible crab has backed its way into a
group of like-coloured pebbles and is now pretending
to be a boulder, remaining motionless with its pincers tucked
under the body. The scalloped edge of
its carapace (shell)
gives it away.

DEADLY STONE
The shallow waters of
Pacific shores can be a
death trap to the
unwary. A stonefish,
which resembles a gnarled
lump of rocky coral, may
suddenly erect the deadly
spines on its back if trodden
on. Its poison can be fatal.

STEADY AS A ROCK
Resembling your surroundings only works
if you stay still like them, or move as they move.
Small shore fish such as the goby (left) and butterfly
blenny (right) remain motionless on the
rocks for long
periods, only
darting off to
chase prey or
avoid predators.

Life on a ledge

A SEABIRD BREEDING COLONY is one of the most spectacular sights on a rocky coastline. Coastal cliffs, rocky islets, and isolated islands are accessible only by flight and so make safe nesting places for birds. Here they are out of reach of all but the most agile ground-based predators, such as snakes and rats, and just beneath the waves there is a rich source of food. The sight of more than 50,000 gannets nesting on an offshore island is breathtaking. The impression is of a blizzard of large white birds coming and going, wheeling on their 1.8 m (6 ft) wings in currents of air, rising up the sheer cliff, regurgitating fish for their chicks, and screeching and pecking at any intruder - gannet or otherwise - that comes within reach of their spear-like bills.

EGG ON A ROCK
The razorbills of the northern hemisphere resemble their southern relatives, the penguins, although unlike penguins they are good fliers. On cliffs they form breeding colonies which may number tens of thousands of birds. Each female lays a single egg.

WARNING
All the eggs shown here come from a museum collection. (The colours have faded slightly.) Collecting or handling wild birds' eggs is now illegal.

EGGS DOWN A HOLE
Puffins nest in burrows. They dig their own holes in soft soil or take over an old shearwater or rabbit tunnel. Puffin eggs are white in colour because, as they are hidden, they have no need of camouflage.

A puffin near a cliff-top burrow by the British bird artist Archibald Thorburn

SUITABLY SHAPED
The blotchily patterned egg of the guillemot is suitably shaped for life on a ledge, as it tapers narrowly to a point at one end. Should it be blown about by the wind or kicked by the bird on the bare rock (the guillemot does not make a nest), it rolls around in a tight circle until it comes to rest.

An adult and a juvenile herring gull by Archibald Thorburn

FIERCE FEEDER
Herring gulls are noisy and aggressive. The squawks and screams from their nesting colonies are deafening. The average clutch consists of three eggs.

Common or great cormorant

Sharp, hooked bill for holding on to slippery prey

A NATURAL FERTILIZER
Guano, the accumulated droppings from a seabird (or bat) colony, is rich in nitrogen, potassium, and phosphorus. Mining guano was a world trade in the last century; most of it came from South American and African coasts and islands, and was shipped to Europe and North America for use as a fertilizer.

DRYING AFTER A DIP
Common or great cormorants are the largest of the 29 species in the cormorant group and are found almost worldwide. They swim and dive after crabs, fish, and other aquatic prey. Afterwards they stand in a typical pose with wings outstretched to dry them. Why cormorants have not evolved water-repellent oils, like many other seabirds, is a mystery.

Long flexible neck for darting at victims

SHIFT WORK
Many cormorants nest by the sea on cliffs, rocky ledges, and sloping stone slabs. Both cormorant parents build their nest from sticks, seaweed, and other locally gathered plant material. The parents take it in turns to incubate their three to five eggs for about one month until the chicks hatch.

All four toes are webbed enabling the cormorant to swim well

Feeding by the sea

Fish are wriggly, slippery creatures. Many animals that catch them have specially adapted mouths so that they can hang on to their awkward prey. Fish-eating mammals such as seals have many small, pointed teeth for this purpose. Fish-eating birds are generally equipped with long, sharp, dagger-like bills (beaks), and the bills of cormorants and many of the gulls also have a down-curved tip to prevent fish from slipping out of the end. Gulls are a familiar sight along the coasts of the northern hemisphere. They hunt along the shore, catching rock-pool fish, pecking at crabs, and hammering open shellfish. Like many other seabirds, they tend to feed near land during the breeding season, but then wander off to lead a mostly pelagic (open-ocean) life for the rest of the year.

AN ALL-PURPOSE BILL
Herring gulls have broad bills, capable of dealing with all kinds of prey, and the contents of rubbish dumps.

SHAPED LIKE A CHISEL
Oystercatchers lever open or hammer through the shells of mussels, cockles, oysters, and other shellfish using their chisel-like bills.

SPEARED FROM ABOVE
The gannet dives from as high as 30 m (100 ft) to catch herring, sardines, mackerel, and other fish. This bird also uses its bill to fight enemies and to stab at those who intrude into its nesting space.

Tube-like nostrils

A HOOKED BILL
Fulmars nest in groups on rocky islands and cliffs. They feed on surface-dwelling fish and their beaks are hooked at the end. They have prominent tube-like nostrils lying along the top or sides of the bill.

Small wings are used as paddles in the water and flap rapidly in flight

DANGEROUS WORK
Seabirds and their eggs are still caught and eaten along some remote shores. On the island of St Kilda, off the northwest coast of Scotland, catches continued to be made until the 1940s. Birds flying past an outcrop were caught in a fleyge net; eggs and nestlings were collected by hand. Gannets, fulmars (right), and various auks were the main victims.

FISHERMAN'S FRIEND
For centuries, coastal people in eastern Asia
have fished with trained cormorants. A
collar and lead is put on the bird, so that it
can catch fish, but not swallow them, and
then be pulled back to the boat.
Today this "fishing" has become
a tourist attraction.

A BILL FULL OF EELS
After a diving session, a catch of up to 10 small fish
(such as these sand eels) is not unusual for the
Atlantic puffin. This bird lives throughout
the North Atlantic.

GOOD FOR SWIMMING
The guillemot or murre (p. 52) has
relatively large, powerful feet with
strong webs. Its legs are positioned
far back along its body so that it
swims efficiently, but
this means that it
waddles, rather
than walks, with
an upright,
penguin-like
stance.

*Guillemot often rests on
"heels" (shanks) on a ledge,
rather than standing*

**SWOOPING
ON THE SHORE**
It is thought that the gull's
pale underside matches the
sky or clouds, making this bird less conspicuous to fish, crabs,
and other prey as they look up, on the watch for danger.
This is a young herring gull with mottled
plumage. Adult birds have
white bellies.

Claw-tipped toes

UNDERWATER PROPELLERS
The gannet's great webbed feet can propel
the bird at remarkable speed under the
water as it chases after fish. It also uses
its feet to cover and help incubate the egg.

*During the breeding
season, the egg (p. 52)
is balanced on the large, webbed feet*

Visitors to the shore

Now and again, we may be lucky enough to see some of the larger visitors to the shore. Marine turtles crawl on to land under cover of darkness to lay their eggs in the warm sand. Seals sunbathe, or the bulls (males) fight each other to gain the right to mate with a harem of females. In the Arctic, white-tusked walruses lie in steaming heaps on the icy rock, while on the Equator, marine iguana lizards crop seaweeds from the rocky shores of the Galapagos Islands. In Antarctica, penguins gather in their millions to rest and breed. However, some visitors to the shore come by accident. The strandings of schools of live whales have long puzzled scientists.

SUN, SEA, AND SAND
During the last century the seaside became popular with one mammal in particular. As is usual with this species, it has greatly changed the habitat. Nowadays, beaches are crowded with its family groups, while the inshore waters are congested with its brightly coloured toys such as yachts and windsurfing boards.

LARDER WITH FLIPPERS
The green turtle, the only plant-eater among the six species of sea-turtles, travels across the world's tropical oceans. Females come ashore to lay eggs in shallow holes scooped in the sand. They tend to use the same beaches, or rookeries, year after year - making it easy for hunters to capture them and steal their eggs. This species grows to 1 m (3 ft) long and 180 kg (400 lb) in weight. It is sometimes called the edible turtle, and in former times it was hunted mercilessly for its flesh, oil, skin, and shell. Today it is officially listed as an endangered species.

STRANDED SQUID
Giant squid, voracious deep-sea predators, are occasionally washed up on the shore. Such stranded individuals are probably injured, ill, or already dead when borne away by shore-bound currents. Giant squid are the largest of all invertebrate animals (those without backbones), growing to more than 15 m (50 ft) in total length and weighing 2 tonnes (tons).

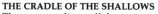

THE CRADLE OF THE SHALLOWS
The sea-otter lives off the coasts of the Pacific Ocean but rarely comes ashore, preferring to lie in the calm of a kelp bed (p. 22). It feeds on sea-urchins, crustaceans, and shellfish, and will use a stone as a tool to crush the hard shells of its prey. This is the heaviest of the 12 otter species, sometimes weighing as much as 45 kg (100 lb). The sea-otter became extremely rare, as it was hunted for its fur, but in 1911 an international agreement (one of the first of its kind) rescued it from extinction.

LIFE ON THE OCEAN WAVE
Common seal pups (these are about three months old) are born on land, but they can swim and dive almost immediately after birth. Seals haul themselves out of the water to bask on rocks and sandbanks, or to give birth. Common seals, which are also called harbour seals, live in coastal waters in the North Pacific and North Atlantic. Recently a viral illness has killed many thousands of those living in the North Sea.

Beachcombing

TWICE EACH DAY the sea rises up the shore and then retreats, depositing debris along the high-tide mark. This is the strandline, a ribbon of objects left stranded high and dry by the tide that is a treasure trove for the nature detective. Shells, bits of seaweed, feathers, and driftwood lie jumbled together, each with a story to tell. Stones, shells, and wood have often been smoothed and sculpted by the sea, rolled to and fro in the sand or crashed against the rocks and split open. Seaweeds torn from rocks are carried along in currents and washed up further along the coast. Large-scale ocean currents such as the Gulf Stream can transport floating objects thousands of kilometres (miles) and dump them on some distant shore. Certain plants use the sea to spread their seeds, the coconut being a famous example. The familiar nut itself ripens inside an even larger husk of stringy grey fibres (the coir, which is made into rough mats and ropes) encased in a brownish leathery skin. This makes a fine "float" and, when a coastal coconut palm drops a husk almost straight into the ocean, it is carried by currents and deposited on a distant shore, where it may grow. In this way coconut palms have spread to fringe tropical shores around the world.

A PEACEFUL PASTIME
Beachcombing is rewarding, as almost anything may be washed up on the shore. In the past people made a living by collecting and selling curios, food, and other objects found on the shore. Today not all shores are suitable for beachcombing as many are strewn with man-made litter, and inshore waters are often polluted.

FOOD FOR FREE
Many seaweeds are gathered for food, both for human and animal consumption (p. 23), and used as fertilizers. Algae such as carragheen are rich in nutrients. For some coastal peoples they are a good source of trace elements, which are minerals that the human body needs in small quantities. Seaweed also has medical applications. Recently a jelly-like seaweed extract used as a lining for bandages for burns has been found to be very effective.

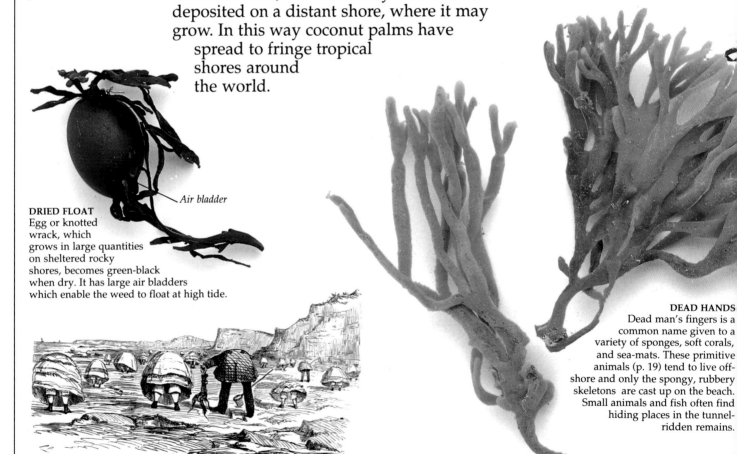

DRIED FLOAT
Egg or knotted wrack, which grows in large quantities on sheltered rocky shores, becomes green-black when dry. It has large air bladders which enable the weed to float at high tide.

Air bladder

DEAD HANDS
Dead man's fingers is a common name given to a variety of sponges, soft corals, and sea-mats. These primitive animals (p. 19) tend to live off-shore and only the spongy, rubbery skeletons are cast up on the beach. Small animals and fish often find hiding places in the tunnel-ridden remains.

A Victorian engraving entitled "Common objects at the sea-side..."

WEAR AND TEAR
Seashells are hard, but no match for the restless waves. Gradually they are ground down and worn away, and the substances from which they are made are returned to the sea.

COMMON COCKLE
Cockles are often found in large numbers in sand or mud.

Netted dog whelks

ERODED PATTERNS
Netted dog whelk shells in various stages of wear.

WORN WHELK
A window has been worn in the largest whorl of this common whelk's shell, revealing its spiral pattern and the central column, the columella.

UPROOTED FROM THE SHORE
This woody object is an underground root, or rhizome, of a giant reed. The reed is the tallest grass in Europe growing to 5 m (15 ft) tall, and is often planted as a wind-break in coastal areas of the Mediterranean. It is also used for making walking sticks, baskets, and fishing rods.

POLISHED BY THE SEA
Bits of slate, glass, and other hard substances are rubbed and polished by sand and water. The scouring action of small sand grains gives a high polish.

BLACK WRACK
This crackly black wrack has been dried through exposure to air. The tiny, coiled, chalky tubes were made by small marine worms, long since perished.

FAN-SHAPED SHELL
This is the flatter, upper valve (p. 26) of a scallop's shell. A fresh specimen's age can be estimated by counting the shell's growth rings. These molluscs may live for more than 15 years.

Hydroides worms often live together, their chalky tubes intertwined on the rocks

Flat winkle (brown)

Flat winkle (yellow)

LESS OF A LIMPET
Limpet rings are a common find. The top of the cone may be pecked and broken by a bird's beak, or bored through by a predatory sea-snail, or cracked off by a boulder.

Sea-mat skeletons

A piece of slate dotted with tiny spirorbid worm tubes and sea-mat skeletons

Remains of shells smoothed and bleached by the sea

"Arms" of sea-urchin

Test of edible sea-urchin

Recently dead sea-urchin with some spines still attached

Hole where the anus was in life

Neck

HOLE IN A STONE
This stone was formed around an animal, the traces of which have long since disappeared.

A FISHY FIND
The skeletons of bony fish such as cod and bass are sometimes cast up on the shore. This broken-up example of a fish shows the rear of the skull and the vertebrae, or backbones, of the neck and main body. These sorts of remains may be the work of fishermen who throw young fish back into the sea

Hole where the mouthparts were in life

HOLES IN THE GLOBE
The sea-urchin's hard, spherical skeleton is called a test (p. 28). The pattern of bumps, hollows, and tiny holes held the spines and tube feet in life, and the large hole contained the anus. Stripped of its spines, the five-rayed symmetry of the animal can be seen, indicating this creature's relationship to the starfish in the echinoderm group. Urchins have been called starfish with "arms" held together over their heads. All the major body organs were enclosed in and protected by the test. They included the roe (the gonads or reproductive parts), which people in some areas collect and eat.

Broad, flattened rear limbs for swimming

Characteristic red joints found on the limbs of this species

Top of carapace detached

Broken parts of ribs

Gills

A gull colony: a mass of noise, droppings, and feathers

Space in centre occupied by heart

FALLING APART AT THE SEAMS
A velvet swimming crab in the early stages of decay has fallen apart at the seams to reveal its internal anatomy. The main organs are contained in the central part of the body. Two large chambers on either side house the gills, with which this crustacean absorbs the oxygen dissolved in seawater.

A FEATHERY FIND
Seabird feathers litter almost every shore, being so light that they float like corks and are easily blown ashore by the wind. Some are from dead birds, but many are simply discarded during the normal plumage moult.

Muscle (meat) in pincer already partly eaten by scavengers

ALL WASHED UP
Pine cones and other light, woody objects may arrive on the seashore after floating down a small stream into a river, and then into the sea.

Mature gull's wing feather

Barred feather typical of young gull

WIND POWER
An onshore wind tends to blow floating items towards the land, improving the beachcomber's chances of finding unusual things.

Cast-up and dried-out young dogfish

Shark in the shallows

The lesser-spotted dogfish, often simply called the dogfish, is a type of shark. It is harmless and grows to about 90 cm (3 ft) in length. Dogfish spend most of their lives offshore, in water around 30-100 m (100-300 ft) deep. However, in late autumn, winter, and spring, females swim into shallow water near the shore to lay their eggs among seaweed.

OUT OF THE CASE
A newly hatched dogfish is about 10 cm (4 in) long. It usually has part of the yolk sac attached, but this shrivels as the youngster begins to feed for itself. When adult, it will hunt bottom-dwelling creatures such as shellfish and other fish.

WATER BABIES
The baby dogfish develop inside their egg cases, each nourished by its yolk sac. They continue to grow for up to 10 months, depending partly on water temperature, before hatching.

BUNDLE OF EGGS
Empty egg cases of the whelk are another common beachcombing find. They are fixed to stones when laid, and tiny but fully formed young whelks crawl out of the cases.

THE MAGIC PURSE
The dogfish egg case is tied to anchoring weed by long tendrils at each corner. Empty cases are often washed up on the shore and are called mermaid's purses.

Studying our shores

WE ENJOY OUR SEASHORES in many different ways. Children paddle in the ripples, surfers ride the waves, naturalists study plants and animals, local people collect seaweed and shellfish for food, and anyone may appreciate the beauty of unspoilt stretches of shore. However, our seashores are being damaged by the increasing pollution of the sea. Throughout history scientists and researchers have studied our shore-lines to understand the way nature works and the way nature is changing. Here we look at some of the tools that have been used in the past and today to help determine the health of our coastlines. We examine the effects of pollution in depth on pages 66–67.

POLLUTION INDICATORS
Some types of seaweeds react quickly to pollution and are termed "indicator species". Records of pressed seashore plants, combined with population surveys of shore inhabitants, help scientists monitor changes over time.

DIVING IN A DUSTBIN
In the 1930s the first scientific surveys of life in the permanent shallows were made. The scientists wore primitive diving hoods equipped with radio telephones. Air was provided by car pumps.

SHELL SHOCK
Shell surveys show how some species have declined with pollution or over-fishing.

SIFTING THROUGH THE SAND
Shrimps, cockles, and other edible shore creatures can be caught along the surf line in wet sand with a strongly made net. The wooden leading edge is pushed just below the surface; sandgrains pass easily through the net, but larger objects are trapped. Shrimping was once a popular pastime and a commercial proposition. Nowadays, many beaches have been over-exploited, or are too polluted or too disturbed by holiday-makers to yield worthwhile catches.

A CLOSER LOOK
The naturalist's indispensible magnifying lens needs a corrosion-proof frame and handle for seashore work.

DE GUIDE
de tables are essential
r anyone who leaves
e main beach to study
cks or flats. As well as dates
d times of low and high water,
e tables give relative water
eights. Look for the lowest spring
de, when the maximum shore
exposed.

OCK RECORD
r scientific studies of the
oreline, a geological map is
ery important. Different types of
cks are colour-coded, and height
ntours are given as on ordinary maps.
ranite, sandstone, and similar hard rocks
nd to form stable rocky shores, while soft
cks like chalk and limestone are
roded more quickly.

RTIST'S INSPIRATION
lany people are fascinated by the
ea; in awe of its destructive power
d attracted by its constant
otion and sudden changes of
ood. Artists have been in-
pired to sketch and paint
numerable beach scenes,
om tranquil summer
ternoons to
rocious winter
orms.

Waterproof torch

LIFE IN THE BALANCE
We cannot see any of
the dissolved
chemicals in
seawater,
but their
levels mean
life or death
for shore creat-
ures. Testing
kits reveal
amounts of
substances, such
as nitrites and nitrates,
that indicate the degree of
pollution present in the seawater.
Large amounts of artificial fertilizers,
which contain nitrogen, are washed into
the sea by rivers carrying soil eroded
from the land. The hydrometer
measures the density or "heavi-
ness" of the seawater, which
reveals the concentration
of dissolved salts.

WATERPROOF EQUIPMENT
Modern waterproof cameras allow us to record
nature without harming it. An underwater
torch is another useful piece of equip-
ment. Many larger animals, such
as lobsters and crabs, hide
themselves in caves and
crevices on the cool,
shadowy side of rocks.
It is always worthwhile
shining a torch before
putting in a hand,
just in case!

LIMPET LEVER
When examining
snails and limpets,
a knife helps to lever
them gently from the
rock. Always put them
back in the same place.

STUDYING
SHORE LIFE
One way of
studying the zon-
ation of life on the
shore (pp. 12-15) is to
stretch a piece of string
down to the sea's edge, if
possible from the high-tide
strandline to the low-tide
mark. Begin at low tide, and
move up the string, recording
the commonest types of seaweeds and
creatures at each stage. Don't forget: after an
hour or so, the tide will start to return.

FASHION OF THE TIME
Fashionable bathing
costumes of the 19th
century may seem
rather quaint today.
But how will today's
costumes be regarded a
century from now?

OUT OF THEIR ELEMENT
Keep shore creatures only for essential
study. They are out of their element: would
you like to be dragged into the sea for an hour?

Did you know?

AMAZING FACTS

 There are around 40,000 species of crustaceans on Earth.

 The biggest bivalve mollusc is the giant clam (*Tridacna gigas*), which is native to the Indo-Pacific Ocean and reaches a weight of around 225 kg (496 lb).

A lobster's blood is colourless. When exposed to oxygen, it develops a bluish colour.

In just one spawning, a shrimp can produce about 500,000 eggs.

Seals swim at an average speed of 19 k/ph (12 mph). Humans swim at less than 1.6 k/ph (1 mph).

The tallest wave ever recorded in the open ocean reached a height of 34 m (112 ft). The wave was recorded by the team of the *USS Ramapo* in the Pacific Ocean in 1933. Tidal waves are produced by earthquakes and can often reach 10 m (33 ft) in height.

Sally lightfoot crabs in the Galapagos

Sally lightfoot crabs do not like being in the water. If forced into the water, they will run across the surface and get out at the first opportunity.

The sea-dwelling snails of the cone shell family include some highly deadly members. Found in tropical regions, these snails carry a poison that is injected by a radula, a mouthpart shaped like a harpoon. This poison can kill a human.

Pea crabs live inside oyster shells and eat food collected by the oyster. Pea crabs damage an oyster's body and are parasites, creatures that live off another living thing without giving anything back.

Spiny starfish

Sea-grasses are the only flowering plants in the sea. They are very important in coastal marine areas, as they are the main diet of dugong and green turtles and provide a habitat for many small marine animals. They also help to gather sediment, (floating particles of mud and soil) and so help to keep the water clear. Australia has the highest number of sea-grass species of any continent.

It takes an average of seven years for a lobster to grow by just 0.45 kg (1 lb) in weight.

Oysters can change from one gender to another and back again, depending on which is best for attracting a mate at that point in time.

Seals are capable of remaining underwater for up to 30 minutes, although they tend to surface after five minutes.

Starfish are the only animals that can turn their stomachs inside out. Some starfish can split their bodies in half and grow new legs to make two whole starfish.

Puffins are incredible divers and can reach depths of 60 m (197 ft) to catch fish. They use their wings to propel themselves underwater and can carry several fish at a time back to the surface.

Climate change experts predict that sea levels may rise by up to 50 cm (19.5 in), by the year 2100, which will increase flooding and coastal erosion.

Waves pick up height and speed from wind

Monaco's coastline is heavily developed

Q Which country has the shortest coastline?

A At just 5.6 km (3.5 miles), Monaco has the shortest coastline of any country. Not surprisingly, as the world's second largest country, Canada has the longest coastline, at 90,908 km (56,487 miles).

Q Is it possible to purify shellfish from sewage-polluted water for safe eating?

A Yes. If shellfish are transplanted from sewage-polluted water to clean water, they have the ability to purify themselves rapidly and so become safe to eat.

Record Breakers

HIGHEST TIDES
• Tides in the Bay of Fundy, Canada, can reach heights of more than 15 m (49 ft).

LARGEST CORAL REEF
• The Great Barrier Reef stretches for 2,028 km (1,260 miles) along the coast of Queensland in northeastern Australia. It covers twice the area of Iceland.

MOST VENOMOUS GASTROPOD
• The most venomous gastropod is the geographer cone shell, found in the Pacific.

BIGGEST CRUSTACEAN
• The Alaskan king crab is the largest crustacean, weighing up to 6.7 kg (15 lb) and measuring around 1.5 m (5 ft) across shell and claws.

LARGEST SEA TURTLE
• The leatherback is the largest of all sea turtles. It can weigh up to 637 kg (1,404 lb) and attain a length of 1.85 m (6 ft).

SALTIEST WATER
• The Red Sea has the saltiest sea water on Earth.

Q What sea creatures are most dangerous to swimmers?

A In some parts of the world sharks pose the main threat to swimmers. Other sea creatures to be avoided include barracudas, moray eels, octopuses, sharp-spined sea urchins, stingrays, toadfish, catfish, and jelly fish. The Portuguese man-of-war has tentacles that can reach 15 m (49 ft) and carry stings that produce painful welts on the human body.

Q How did European ponies end up on the island of Assateague in the USA?

A There is mystery surrounding how the population of wild ponies came to be on the island of Assateague in Maryland, Virginia, USA. The recent discovery of a sunken shipwreck near the island has given rise to the theory that a Spanish ship with a cargo of horses sank off the coast in the 1600s. Some horses swam ashore and have continued to breed down through the years. There is now a robust population of around 300.

Wild ponies on Assateague Island

Q How do oysters produce pearls?

A A pearl begins when a foreign substance, such as a grain of sand, enters an oyster shell. The oyster's body reacts by depositing material around the foreign body to wall it off and reduce irritation. Over the years these deposits build up to create a pearl.

Q Where do sea turtles breed?

A Sea turtles live most of their lives in the ocean, but nesting females return to the beach where they were born. They must often travel very long distances from their feeding grounds to lay their eggs.

Q Do fish ever sleep?

A Fish do not sleep in the same way as humans, but they do rest. Fish cannot close their eyes, and some fish never stop moving. However, most fish have rest periods when they just float or nest in a quiet spot, while remaining semi-alert.

Protecting our coastlines

POLLUTION OF THE WORLD'S COASTLINES is an increasing threat to the animals and plants that live on the shoreline. Here we examine some of the effects of coastal pollution. We also look at some of the types of coastline that exist as a reminder of the delicate beauty that needs to be preserved. You can help protect seashore wildlife. As a visitor to the beach, always take your waste away and try to not disturb plants and animals. Find out if there are local volunteer schemes that you can join, or perhaps start a research project at your school.

TOURISM
The Mediterranean sea turtle is under threat. These turtles need access to quiet beaches on which to lay their eggs, but many beaches have been overrun by tourism. Conservation projects, such as the one shown above, help to save turtles.

Discharge of sewage off the Mediterranean coast

SEWAGE WASTE
Around the world millions of tonnes of sewage and industrial waste are discharged into the oceans every day. Sewage and chemicals affect aquatic habitats and poison plant and animal life, also making the seas unsafe for humans to swim in.

OVERFISHING
In most parts of the world the rate of commerical fishing is so high that fish populations are not being given a chance to breed and maintain their numbers. The levels of most species of marine fish are at an all-time low.

OIL SPILLAGES
When ships carrying oil suffer a spillage, the effects for a marine ecosystem are disastrous. Birds, fish, and plants that come into contact with the oil will be poisoned and often perish. These puffins were contaminated by an oil slick and died.

Nets can trap other fish as well as the intended catch

A haul of salmon

SEA TRAFFIC

Development along coastlines, such as ports, can wipe out natural habitats. Even without accidents, normal ship operations discharge a great deal of oil into the sea. Salerno port in Italy, shown here, is divided into a fishing port and a tourist port, both of which have hundreds of ships coming and going daily.

BEACH POLLUTION

As package holidays and travelling become more popular, so are the world's beaches being slowly ruined. Sunbathers leave plastic water bottles and other waste on the beach. Applied suncreams also wash off in the water and build up chemical residues.

SHORELINE HABITATS

SHINGLE

A shingle beach is made up of pebbles or stones. This is one of the least hospitable beach habitats, as most plants and animals find it difficult to survive the constant disruption of the stones being moved by the tides. This shingle is from the Sussex coast in England.

BASALT

A basalt or black sand beach is made up of volcanic lava that has been broken down into fine grains by the waves over the years. This type of beach is quite rare, but there are stunning examples around the world, such as this one in Iceland.

White sand beach, Tanzania

WHITE SAND

This is the most popular type of beach for holidaymakers. White sand is rock, shells, or coral that have been ground into very fine particles and bleached by hot sun. Soft sand makes a welcoming home for burrowing animals and insects, and also allows predators easy access to them for food.

ROCKY SHORE

Rocky shores are made up of rock pools, boulder fields, and flat rock platforms. A great diversity of plant and animal life thrives on these shores. Rock pools are mini marine ecosystems, boulders offer shelter from weather, and platforms are home to species that need to stay dry. The shore above is in the Canadian Arctic.

Find out more

EVERY SHORELINE IS ABUNDANT with plant and animal life for you to discover. Just by walking along the beach you will come across plenty of interesting specimens. Explore shallow waters or rock pools with a net. Behind the beach, cliffs, caves, sand dunes, and salt marshes are home to many more plants and creatures. To learn about seashore life in different parts of the world, visit a marine aquarium or a natural history museum.

SNORKELLING
One of the best ways to find out about the plants and creatures that live on the shoreline is to go snorkelling. Accompanied by an adult, choose a rock-free stretch of water to swim in. Look out for fish, coral, plants, and pretty shells.

USEFUL WEBSITES

- British Marine Life Study Society: seashore page
  ourworld.compuserve.com/homepages/BMLSS/ seashore.htm
- Ocean.com: good guide to marine mammals, fishes, birds, invertebrates, plants, algae, and reptiles
  www.ocean.com/Library/CreatureFeature/default.asp
- Seashells.org: How to identify, clean, and care for shells
  www.seashells.org
- Kids Do Ecology: Marine Mammal Pages
  www.nceas.ucsb.edu/nceas-web/kids/mmp/home.htm

Mask and snorkel allow you to see and breathe face down in the water

Places to visit

LONDON AQUARIUM, LONDON, ENGLAND, UK
• Exhibitions on worldwide seashores, covering everything from rock pools to coral reefs.

NATURAL HISTORY MUSEUM, LONDON, ENGLAND, UK
• There are galleries dedicated to fossil marine reptiles, marine invertebrates, and marine fish.

EXMOOR NATIONAL PARK AUTHORITY, SOMERSET, ENGLAND, UK
• Take part in the park's organized walks, which include seaside safaris on Lynmouth Beach and nature exploration outings.

BLUE PLANET AQUARIUM, CHESHIRE, ENGLAND, UK
• A voyage of discovery that will take you round the world, evoking the steamy coastal mangroves and crashing surf of the Caribbean.

RAMSEY ISLAND NATURE RESERVE, PEMBROKESHIRE, WALES, UK
• Stunning cliff scenery, a diverse marine bird population, and one of the UK's largest communities of Atlantic grey seals.

MARINE AQUARIUM
Most cities have a marine aquarium which is home to hundreds of amazing sea creatures from around the world. During your visit find out which plants and creatures exist far out at sea and which can be found living near the shoreline.

BEACHCOMBING
Any stroll along the shore will throw up an array of plants and creatures washed up by the tide. Look out for shells, seaweed, jellyfish, and coral. Insects and burrowing creatures will be teeming just beneath the surface of any sandy beach. Close to rocks, you may find scuttling crabs and clinging shellfish.

ROCK POOLING
The best time to explore rock pools is at low tide, which happens twice a day. You can find out times by looking at tide tables and asking locally. Take a net to help you catch your finds and a margarine tub or bucket to temporarily hold them. You may discover crabs, fish, seaweed, starfish, and much more.

PLANT DISCOVERY
Coastal plants must be hardy to survive the extreme weather conditions that occur on exposed land. Salt marshes that form on lowlands behind the shore can be home to an array of sea-grasses and rushes. Flowering plants are often found in sheltered spots.

BIRD WATCHING
There are many types of fascinating birds to be studied on the coast. As well as the ever-present gulls, you will see waders probing in the sand for food with their long beaks during low tides. Many birds make their nests on the cliffs, where they are relatively safe from humans and predators.

Glossary

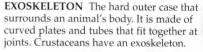

A crab is
a crustacean

ANTENNAE The sensory organs on each side of the head, also called feelers, or horns. Antennae can have many functions, including navigation, taste, sight, and hearing. Crabs, lobsters, and prawns all have antennae.

ARTHROPOD A member of a major division of the animal kingdom with a segmented body and joined appendages (limbs), such as a crustacean or an insect.

BIVALVE An animal with a shell in two parts or valves, such as an oyster or mussel.

CALCAREOUS A substance containing or composed of calcium carbonate, such as chalk or limestone. Cliffs are often calcareous.

CAMOUFLAGE The means by which an animal escapes the notice of predators, usually because it blends in with its surroundings.

CARAPACE The hard shield that covers the bodies of crabs, lobsters, and shrimps. The top part of a turtle's shell is also called a carapace.

CHELIPED The claw-bearing appendage (limb) of a crustacean.

CHLOROPHYLL The green pigment present in most plants and central to photosynthesis, a process in which plants use sunlight to create their own food.

COELENTERATE A water-dwelling invertebrate, usually with a simple tube-shaped body. Jellyfish, corals, and sea anemones are all coelenterates, or cnidarians.

Tropical fish can only live in a warm habitat

CORAL A small sea animal that catches food with stinging tentacles. Many corals live in large colonies called coral reefs.

CORRASION The grinding up of the Earth's surface when rock particles are carried over it by pounding waves.

CRUSTACEAN An invertebrate with jointed legs and two pairs of antennae.

DORSAL FIN The fin located at the back or rear of a fish's body.

ECOLOGY The study of the relationship between living things and their environment.

ECHINODERM A sea animal with an internal skeleton and a body divided into five equal parts, such as a starfish.

ENDANGERED When the numbers of a species are so low that it may become extinct.

EROSION The wearing away of rock or soil by the gradual detachment of fragments by water, wind, and ice.

ESTUARY The wide, lower tidal part of a river where it flows into the ocean.

EXTINCTION The permanent disappearance of a species, nowadays often as a result of hunting or pollution.

EXOSKELETON The hard outer case that surrounds an animal's body. It is made of curved plates and tubes that fit together at joints. Crustaceans have an exoskeleton.

FAUNA The animal life found in a particular habitat.

FLORA The plant life found growing in a particular habitat.

FOSSIL The remains or traces of a living thing preserved in rock.

FROND A leaf or leaf-like part of a sea plant, sometimes frilled at the edges.

FUCOXANTHIN A brown pigment or colour in sea plants such as kelp. This pigment masks out chlorophyll, the green pigment present in most plants.

Scarlet ibis, found among coastal fauna of northern South America

GASTROPOD A class of assymetrical molluscs, including limpets, snails, and slugs, in which the foot is broad and flat and the shell, if any, is in one piece and conical.

GRANITE A rough-grained igneous rock that originally formed deep inside the Earth.

HABITAT The physical environment or normal abode of a plant or animal.

HIGH TIDE The highest point reached on the shore when the tide is in.

HOLDFAST A branched structure on a sea plant that fixes itself to a rock and keeps the plant stable in one spot. A holdfast is sometimes also called a hapteron.

HOST A living thing that provides food and a home for a parasite.

IGNEOUS Any rock solidified from molten material, such as lava.

INTERTIDAL ZONE The area on a beach that lies between the highest and lowest points reached by the tides.

INVERTEBRATE An animal that has no backbone.

KELP A type of seaweed, often brown and with a holdfast.

LAVA Most commonly refers to streams of hot liquid rock that flow from a volcano, but also refers to this rock when it has cooled and solidified.

LOW TIDE The lowest point reached on the shore when the tide is out.

LUNG A body organ used to breathe air.

MIDRIB A central stem in the leaf of a plant.

MIGRATION A journey by an animal to a new habitat. Many animals make a regular migration each year to feed or breed.

MINERALS A naturally occurring inorganic substance, which is usually hard. Most rocks are made from minerals.

MUTUALISM A close relationship between two species in which both partners benefit. Clownfish and sea anemones have such a relationship by providing each other with protection from predators.

NEAP TIDE A tide that occurs every 14–15 days and coincides with the first and last quarters of the moon. This tide does not reach very high up or low down the shore.

ORGANISM A living thing.

PARASITE An organism that spends part or all of its life in close association with another species, taking food and shelter from it, but giving nothing in return.

PEDICELLARIA Sharp, beak-like structures that cover the surface of some echinoderms, such as sea urchins. Pedicellaria are used for both feeding and protection.

PHYCOERYTHRIN A red pigment or colour in sea plants such as kelp that masks out the green pigment chlorophyll.

Plankton with animal and plant components

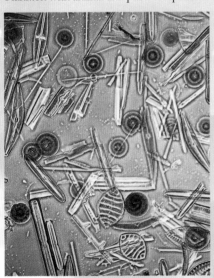

Like all bivalves, mussels are invertebrates

PLANKTON Minute organisms, including animal and algae, that are found in the surface layers of water. Plankton drift with the current.

POLLUTION Disruption of the natural world by chemicals and other agents.

PREDATOR An animal that hunts other animals for food.

PREY The animals that are hunted and eaten by a predator.

SCAVENGER An animal that feeds on dead plants or animals.

SEDIMENT Light rock particles that settle on the ocean floor. Sea water becomes cloudy when this sediment is stirred up.

SERRATED A sharply toothed surface, much like a saw.

SHALE A type of rock that forms from hardened particles of clay.

SILT Tiny particles of rock and mineral that can form the ocean bed.

SPECIES A group of living things that can breed together in the wild.

SPRING TIDE A tide pattern that occurs every 14–15 days at full and new moons, when the tide reaches the highest up and the lowest down the shore.

Clownfish and anemones, mutually beneficial

STIPE The stalk, or stem, of a plant.

STRANDLINE The line of washed-up shells, seaweed, drift wood, and other debris left on the beach when the tide has gone out.

STRATUM A layer, usually of rock.

SYMBIOSIS A close living relationship between two different species that often depend on each other for survival.

TEMPERATE A type of climate on Earth, characterized by moderate conditions.

TOPSHELL A short cone-shaped shell belonging to a sea-dwelling gastropod.

WADER A bird that searches for food on the shoreline, usually by standing in shallow water and probing its long beak into the sand for insects and worms.

WRACK One of the main types of seaweed, usually brown in colour, and tough and slippery in texture.

VEGETATION The plants that grow in a particular habitat.

VENOM A poisonous substance in an animal's bite or sting.

VERTEBRATE An animal that has a backbone. There are five main groups of vertebrates: fish, amphibians, reptiles, birds, and mammals.

Sea-grass is common to coastal vegetation

Index

Acknowledgements

The author and Dorling Kindersley would like to thank:

Dr Geoff Potts and the Marine Biological Association of the United Kingdom.
The Booth Museum of Natural History, Brighton, for supplying the specimens on pages 52–55.
Trevor Smith's Animal World.
Collins and Chambers.
Wallace Heaton, Jane Williams, Jonathan Buckley, Barney Kindersley and Dr David George, Dr Paul Cornelius, Dr Bob Symes, David Moore, Ian Tittley, Arthur Chater, Dr Ray Ingle, Gordon Patterson, Dr John Taylor, Solene Morris, Susannah van Rose, Alwyne Wheeler, Chris Owen and Colin Keates of the Natural History Museum.
Richard Czapnik for help with design.
Ella Skene for the index.
Victoria Sorzano for typing.
Fred Ford of Radius Graphics for artwork.
David Burnie for consultancy.

Picture credits
t = top; b = bottom; m = middle; l = left; r = right

Heather Angel: 12br, 23ml, 30tr, 42tl & b, 49br, 69tl
Ardea London Ltd: 54bl
Atlantide SNC/Bruce Coleman Ltd: 67b
Leo Batten/FLPA – Images of Nature: 69c
Erik Bjurstrom/Bruce Coleman Ltd: 70bl
Liz and Tony Bomford/Ardea London Ltd: 66 cr
B Borrell/FLPA: Images of Nature, 66c
Mark Boulton/Bruce Coleman Ltd: 8tl
Professor George Branch: 12b
Jane Burton/Bruce Coleman Ltd: 45tl
Bob & Clara Calhoun/Bruce Coleman Ltd: 37m, 43m
N Callow/NHPA: 31
G J Cambridge/NHPA: 15m
Laurie Campbell/NHPA: 24t
James Carmichael Jr/NHPA: 49bl
C Carvalho/Frank Lane: 23mr
Judith Clarke/Bruce Coleman Ltd: 71br
Eric Crichton/Bruce Coleman Ltd: 20tl
Nicolas Devore/Bruce Coleman Ltd: 9m
Adrian Evans/Hutchison Library: 10m
Mary Evans Picture Library: 8m, 14tl, 18

& 19b, 20b, 23tr, 26tl, 27, 30tl, 36, 38tl, 47tr, 53tl, 55tl, 56tr & m, 58bl, 59tr
Kenneth W Fink/Ardea London Ltd: 56bl
Jeff Foott/Bruce Coleman Ltd: 24b, 30ml, 31bl
Neville Fox-Davies/ Bruce Coleman Ltd: 25m
J Frazier/NHPA: 50tr
Pavel German/NHPA: 50tr
Jeff Goodman/NHPA: 40mr & br
Robert Francis/Robert Harding Picture Library: 67tr
Mark E Gibson/Corbis: 68bl
Francois Gohier/Ardea London Ltd: 69r
Chris Gomersall/Bruce Coleman Ltd: 71tc
P Guegan/Sunset/FLPA: 67tl
Ian Griffiths/Robert Harding Picture Library: 17br
Tony Hamblin/FLPA: 69bl
Robert Harding Picture Library: 9b, 11bl
Michael Holford/Victoria and Albert Museum: 26br
Scott Johnson/NHPA: 31br, 48m
Tony Jones/Robert Harding: 11tr
M P Kahl/Bruce Coleman Ltd: 8bl
Franz Lanting/Bruce Coleman Ltd: 12tl
Richard Matthews/Seaphot Ltd: Planet Earth Pictures: 55m

Marine Biological Association of the United Kingdom: 62tr
John Mitchell/Oxford Scientific Films: 66t
Mark Newman/FLPA: 67cl
M Nimmo/Frank Lane: 8tr
Fritz Polking GDT/Frank Lane: 44m, 61
Dr Geoff Potts: 30b
Mike Price/SAL/Oxford Scientific Films: 65br
Niall Rankin/Eric Hosking: 54br
Joel W Rogers/Corbis: 66b
Walter Rohdich/FLPA: 65t
Ann Ronan Picture Library: 8br
John Taylor/Bruce Coleman Ltd: 43br
Kim Taylor/Bruce Coleman Ltd: 39tr
Roger Tidman/Frank Lane: 10tr
M I Walker/NHPA: 71bl
W Wisniewski/FLPA: 67
Norbert Wu/NHPA: 64b
Bill Wood/NHPA: 40ml
Gunter Ziesler/Bruce Coleman Ltd: 29ml

All other images © Dorling Kindersley.
For further information see:
www.dkimages.com

Illustrations by: John Woodcock
Picture research by: Elizabeth Eyres